HINDU GODS AND GODDESSES

 **DIAMOND BOOKS**

© Publisher

Published 2008
By
DIAMOND POCKET BOOKS (P) LTD.
X-30, Okhla Industrial Area
Phase-2, New Delhi 110020
Phone 011-41611861-865
Fax-011-26386124, 41611866
e-mail: sales@dpb.in
www.dpb.in

Design: Ritu Sinha

ISBN-81-288-0802-8

Publishers
Printed in India by
Best Photo offset
New Delhi, India

ACKNOWLEDGEMENT

I would like to thank my daughter-in-law Reenu son Alok and my son-in-law Rohit & daughter Alka who all belong to the Generation X and are also NRIs, for giving me the basic concept and an idea about the format for this work, which would be relevant and interesting to young persons like them.

I am also indebted to my wife Shobha for her overall management of this project, with whose support this effort has borne fruit.

Above all, I am grateful to my co-author Mr. B.K. Chaturvedi who is so masterly in this field of knowledge and very modern in his approach. Without his unstinted support, this exercise might not have been so authentic.

I dedicate this book to the memory of my father Mr.O.N.Mathur(Bagchi Saheb) who left for his heavenly abode during printing of this book.

Suresh Narain Mathur

INTRODUCTION

Hindu mythology is the world's richest collection of stories about supernatural personalities and events, both in terms of volume and quality, written and re-written by several scholars spread over pre-historic periods and later.

Consequently, it is somewhat incoherent and confusing to common persons, particularly the Generation X. This treatise attempts to put much of the popularly available information in a nutshell and more particularly in an executive style and in a very simple language for ease of reading and understanding. This should particularly suit Generation X/NRIs. Moreover, we have tried to stick to popularly accepted details and avoided controversial details.

Despite its origin in a hoary past, Hindu mythology gives certain concepts which are new even to modern sciences. Like the concept of relativity of time. Although Albert Einstein proved it at the beginning of the 20th century, Hindu mythology always maintained time's existence in duality, divine-years vis-a-vis man-years.

Moreover, as early as in the times of Vedas compilation, scholars knew that Moon has only reflected light and the real source of its light is the Sun. They knew about the seven heavenly bodies: Sun, Moon, Mars, Mercury, Jupiter, Venus and Saturn. They had not only conceptualised the aerial vehicle-Vimans- but had also divised one called Pushpak Viman. But all the missing links got lost in the antiquity of time.

Today, lives of Hindus are saturated with religion and associated rituals as well as belief in several related concepts.

Recent projection of serials on Hindu Gods & Goddesses on TV has aroused interest in people who want their information on Hindu mythology simple and clear. It is towards this objective that this attempt has been made to provide a simple overview.

It is understood that there are 330 million gods & goddesses in Hindu mythology. Here we have tried to list only the more popular ones, for sake of convenience and being brief.

New Delhi

Suresh Narain Mathur
B.K. Chaturvedi

FIRST INFORMATION SHEET FOR THE READER

1. Names of all the gods/goddesses and some other terms in this book have been spelled as per common pronunciation, typically doing away with the last alphabet 'a' like in Ganesh'a' as spelled in an anglicised manner.

2. 'Ji' has been added as suffix to the names of most of the gods/goddesses as their names are always pronounced by devout Hindus, conveying respect.'Ji' is a corrupted form of the term 'Arya' which was used as a prefix to names, by Aryans to convey respect.'Arya' got changed to 'Aji' and finally to'Ji' as a suffix.

3. This text, in some instances, may contain contradictory/differing versions of the same event. This is because the same event may be described in different ways in different scriptures.

4. Some better known/understood Hindi (Indian language) words appear italicised

5. Whenever word 'man' or 'his' appear, it may please be considered as applicable to both the genders.

6. Disclaimer - Information provided in this book is based on mythology/available information and is given here in good faith. This information may be used for help to reckoning only.

7. Text- copyright @ Suresh Narain2003

CONTENTS

वक्रतुण्ड महाकाय सूर्यकोटिसमप्रभः।
निर्विघ्नं कुरु मे देव सर्वकार्येषु सर्वदा।।

**Vakratunda mahakaya suryakoti samaprabha
nirvighnam kurme dev sarva karyeshu sarvada**

Oh lord the Almighty! Relieve us from various natural calamities and make us successful forever through your huge body, larger trunk and the brilliance of million suns in the solar system.

GANESH JI
AN IMPORTANT ETERNAL HINDU GOD

Vidya-Varidhi & Buddhi Vidhata
(This is how Ganesh Ji described in religious scriptures)

It is interesting to observe that Ganesh Ji's image appears on the opening page of this book. Hindu mythology offers some interesting stories giving reasons for this pre-eminence to Ganesh Ji. One such story is as follows. Once when Ganesh Ji's mother, goddess Parvati Ji desired to have bath and have privacy for that purpose, she created Ganesh Ji from her sweat and asked him to keep guard. After sometime, Parvati Ji's husband Shiv Ji returned but was denied entry by this guard Ganesh Ji since he was not aware of Shiv Ji's identity. This infuriated Shiv Ji who cut-off Ganesh Ji's head. When Parvati Ji arrived on the scene and explained that Ganesh Ji was her off-spring, Shiv Ji felt very sorry. He sent his attendants to search for a child's head, a child whose mother should be asleep so that she does not have to go through the torture of separation from her child. These attendants found a young elephant in such a position and brought it to Shiv Ji, who then transplanted this young elephant's head onto Ganesh Ji's body and brought him back to life. But Parvati Ji was still annoyed with the whole episode. At this juncture, Brahma Ji had also arrived on the scene and granted a very special boon in favour of Ganesh Ji, to please Parvati Ji, that Ganesh Ji will henceforth be the first among all gods and will receive top eminence in case of worship. More details on Ganesh Ji are given in the chapter devoted to him.

EXISTENCE OF GOD

& MAN'S RELATIONSHIP WITH HIM

Inspite of being invisible, having no eyewitnesses and beyond the conventionally accepted facts, an extremely over-whelming majority of mankind all over the world believes in the existence of God. According to the scientific community, there is vast, rather divine energy beyond the realm of time and space, which causes formation of galaxies, stars, worlds, living beings and all other things which are governed by certain rhythms.

Hence, in absence of availability of clear facts, all the religions were woven around mythology propounded by the old and the wise philosophers. Much of Hinduism and the myths around it, took shape with the advent of Aryan race which came to this land from Caucasian region, sometime around 5000-3000 BC.

Influenced by the aboriginals of the land whose culture might have been limited to rituals to propitiate animals and spirits of the dead and by Dravidians who believed in things symbolic of God's creation as perceived at that time, Aryans propagated natural elements like earth *(Bhoomi)*, sky *(Gagan)*, air *(Vayu)*, fire *(Agni)* and water *(Neer)*, giv-ing rise to the concept of almighty, naming him *Bhagvan*. Hymns in praise of these elements were composed, such

TO ACHIEVE ULTIMATE PEACE, AS KRISHNJI PRONOUNCED IN GITA⁴, THERE ARE THREE ROUTS

GYAN MARG : **ACQUIRING KNOWLEDGE AND SPREADING IT**
The route typically taken by saints and scholars. Examples are Kabir, Guru Nanak etc.

KARM MARG : **DOING GOOD TO OTHERS**
The route typically taken by reformers and good samaritans. Examples are Swami Dayannd, Gandhi etc. who actively contributed towards improving the society as a whole. This found support of Buddha also.

BHAKTI MARG : **DEVOTION TO GOD**
The route typically taken by holy personalities like Meera, Surdas , Tulsidas etc. to instil faith among people in general.

as *Gayatri Mantr* in literature being written at that time, namely the *Vedas*. This literature provided fillip to the concept of God's different manifestations, like *Vayu Dev, Surya Dev* etc. Popularisation of Vedic literature gave rise to belief in the existence of God the creator, God the preserver and God the destroyer. With difficult periods showing up regularly in the form of invaders, the concept of reincarnation of Gods took shape. And finally, each individual chose his own personal God, suiting his own predispositions and personality.

As clarified in the following chapter *(Om)*, choosing of personal God has been a matter of convenience for realisation of *Sagun* God (with form) as against the relatively difficult realisation of *Nirgun* God (without form), the supreme power. According to Hindu belief, where the concept of *Atma* being indestructible is deep rooted, every individual aspires to ultimately merge with this supreme power and be emancipated.

Each individual has to choose one or more ways to achieve ultimate peace. A real saint or Guru can be helpful in determining this, depending on individual's predispositions & personality.

It may be in the fitness of things to add here that since all mythologies are based on folk tales, full of fiction, Hindu mythology and its constituent details on gods & goddesses should not be put to scientific test/logic, but be looked at as they are.

Another interesting feature of a Hindu's relationship with his gods/goddesses is that each individual establishes a direct and personal relationship with them. To facilitate this relationship, images of all gods/goddesses have specially large and penetrating eyes. As a consequence, Hindus are generally introvert, concentrating more on themselves and their gods/goddesses and less on the surroundings and the society.

POPULARLY WOSHIPPED

HINDU GODS & GODDESSES

As mentioned earlier, lives of Hindus are saturated with religion, which entails worship of several gods & goddesses and following of several rituals and festivals. Although monotheism is the basic philosophy in Hindusim and remains more on a theoretical level, for practical purposes our sages later developed the manifestation concept.

In line with this concept, God was realised as *trimurti*, comprising the creator, the preserver and the destroyer in the perpetual cycle of the creation-destruction- recreation of the universe. Also, the idea of *avataars* (reincarnation) of some of the gods & goddesses appeared on the horizon, as redeemers gave a substantial feeling of comfort to those Hindus who had to face oppression by invaders and/or cruel rulers.

Although the number of Hindu gods & goddesses is said to be over 330 million, the visual here gives only the commonly popular and eternal gods & goddesses, their hierarchy and some of their *avataars*. Idea is to avoid scholarly details and ensure clarity in the minds of the ones who wish to reckon details of primary relevance first.

"OM"

GOD AS *NIRGUN*

Om is the mystic and holy word which sums up all truth in the universe. According to Hindu mythology, which is understood to have a beginning over 5000 years ago, God is -

*OM*NIPRESENT meaning present everywhere.
*OM*NISCIENT meaning infinitely knowledgeable and
*OM*NIPOTENT meaning infinitely powerful.
(Mark the prefix *'Om'* in all these epithets for God.)

God is thus, eternal, formless and the Absolute soul Paramatma, the supreme energy which controls the whole universe. Om (or Aum) symbolises God as nirgun, meaning without form, the Absolute.
Om is pronounced at the beginning and /or end of rituals and prayers. This pronouncing is understood to create vibrations which link up with the supreme energy *Parmatma*, the life source of all creation in the universe.

One school of thought has it that earlier *Aryans* worshipped natural elements namely:-
1. *Bhoomi* (earth)
2. *Gagan* (sky/space)
3. *Vayu* (air)
4. *Agni* (fire) and
5. *Neer* (water)

Brahma Ji
who creates everything

Vishnu Ji
who protects good people

Shiv Ji
who destroy evil

giving rise to the term Bhagvan for this supreme energy.

To make it convenient to comprehend the nirgun, forms with different attributes evolved as sagun-meaning with form. God with such forms would then help a person during his/her existence, when propitiating these gods through good *karm* (deeds). It also helps one to look at the sagun reality, attributes of which suit one from one's viewpoint, as evolved during one's personality growth.

To make one understand *nirgun & sagun* aspects, **Ramkrishn Paramhans** used to give example of water, which is *nirgun* in its usual form and sagun when in snow/ice form.

According to Hindu mythology the

supreme energy as *sagun*, is *Trimurty* (Trinity), an immense energy which controls the universe and its activities. Another all-permeating aspect of *nirgun* form of God is *Sat, Chit & Anand*, meaning the 3 basic attributes of the Supreme i.e. truth, consciousness and blissfulness.

While Brahma Ji is not popular in present day (he is understood to have completed his task of creation of the universe and made it a self-continuing process), Vishnu Ji and Shiv Ji are popularly worshipped, respectively as the sustainer of the creation and its destruction when it has outlived its utility. There are other gods/goddesses who are adored and they are described in some detail in the following chapters.

VISHNU JI
NUMERO UNO AMONG GODS, WHO PROTECTS

Vishnu Ji is the preserver of creation. Whenever anyone dares disturb the rules of conduct, He incarnates himself to remove those devils. He is also the only god among the trinity who never grants any boon to devils. As against this, Brahama Ji as well as Shiv Ji have been liberal on this count of granting boons to devils who worship them and subsequently become very powerful and have ultimately to be annihilated by Vishnu Ji in his several incarnations.

ORIGIN

Vishnu Ji is eternal and the supreme power. Actually formless (nirgun), he acquires forms with different attributes which make it convenient for humans to comprehend him.

The name Vishnu Ji is derived from the word vish[1], which spreads in all directions, indicative of Vishnu Ji's omnipresence.

ABODE

Omnipresent, but his favourite place is Vaikunth (heaven) identified with fabled *Ksheer Sagar*[2]. It is an ultimate Abode, which humans aspire to reach, through good deeds.

IMPORTANCE

As the supreme eternal God, who protects, the absolute universal soul Parmatma, he protects his devotees and ensures good moral order in the universe.

He is infinitely powerful *(Omnipotent)*
Present everywhere *(Omnipresent)* and
Infinitely knowledgeable *(Omniscient)*.

The entire universe is a revelation of him, from whom evolve all forms of life as well as everything material. He is regarded as highly charitable and rewarding to his devotees, resulting in his high popularity and acceptance as the most powerful god in this increasingly materialistic world.

His protecting powers have been demonstrated in several forms/ incarnations - *avataars*[3], to destroy evil and bring good order on earth. Commonly understood and accepted as ten incarnations, these are described in some detail in a separate chapter in this book.

SOME OTHER NAMES / EPITHETS

1. Bala Ji
2. Chaturbhuj
3. Hari
4. Janardan
5. Narain
6. Padmanabh
7. Ranganath
8. Satya Narain
9. Venkateshwar
10. Vardaraj
11. Vaikunthnath

TYPICAL DEPICTION

1. Resting on the coiled serpent deity Sheshnag[4], on the ocean surface, holding in his four hands
- *Conch (shankh called Panchjanya)*
- *Discus (Sudershan Chakra)*
- *Lotus (kamal flower, Padma)*

or arrows, quiver and bow (named Saranga) alongwith Lakshmi Ji, his wife seated alongside, gently pressing his feet to impart feeling of comfort. Usually also shown, is a lotus flower emanating from Vishnu Ji's navel, with Brahma Ji seated on it.

2. Vishnu Ji, standing on water waves, accompanied by wife Lakshmi Ji and holding in his hands, items as enumerated earlier.

3. Sitting together with Lakshmi Ji, on the divine eagle Garud, again holding the same four items in his hands.

Vishnu Ji is generally depicted as blue-skinned, wearing regal ornaments and yellow garments.

Like in case of Vishnu Ji, most Hindu gods are shown with several arms, symbolising their manifold powers. It is also worthwhile to note that Lakshmi Ji, like wife of any other god, is always shown on Vishnu Ji's left side.

SOME TEMPLES
- Venkateshwara Bala Ji (Thirumala Thirupati, A.P.)
- Padmanabh Temple (Thiruvananthapuram, Kerala)
- Ranganath of Srirangam (Thiruchirapali, TN)
- Vaikunthnath Hari Ram Temple (Chamba, HP)
- Varadaraj (Kanchipuram TN)
- Badrinath Temple (Badrinath, Uttaranchal)

RELATED FESTIVALS CEREMONIES
- *Satya Narain Ji Ki Katha*
- *Ram Navmi, Janam Ashtmi* etc. which signify the birth of his incarnations.

SOME INTERESTING INFORMATION
- Worshippers of Vishnu Ji (exclusively), are called Vaishnavs, originating in TN around 1500 AD.
- 6 of the 18 Puranas are addressed to Vishnu Ji.
- On Vishnu Ji's advice, gods and demons undertook churning of the ocean, Samudra Manthan. From this process of ocean churning, came out 14 precious gems etc. Out of these Vishnu Ji claimed four items for himself, namely the conch *(shankh)*, the bow *(Saranga)*, the mace *(gada)* and the jewel Kaustabha. Lakshmi Ji who also emerged from this process, was a gift to Vishnu Ji as his wife.
- Vishnu Ji also appeared as Mohini, celestial dancer, during samudra manthan, to lure away demons from partaking nectar- amrit.

LAKSHMI JI
GODDESS OF FORTUNE & WIFE OF VISHNU JI

Typically all the gods & goddesses acquire a certain exalted status because of one or more legends in support their supernatural powers.However, it is an exception in case of Lakshmi Ji. She only accompanies her spouse Vishnu Ji during his several incarnations and other occasions.Lakshmi Ji symbolises availability of material resources, hence it is logical for the god, responsible for maintaining order and propriety in the world, to have her as constant companion.

ORIGIN
Lakshmi Ji emerged from ocean at the end of a series of precious gems etc. during *samudra manthan*. She was hiding there in the ocean out of fear of the curse of sage Bhrigu who had passed a curse on all celestial beings. She was gifted to Vishnu Ji as his wife, a reward from gods for Vishnu Ji's efforts in diverting demons away from partaking

amrit. She is held to be the Goddess of all riches and affluence.

Whenever Vishnu Ji incarnates himself on earth, Lakshmi Ji appears with him, in order to be with him and assist him. Like Vishnu Ji, she is also eternal and omnipresent.

According to one interpretation in mythology, *Maa Shakti* or *Maha Maya*, representing *Sat, Chitt & Anand*, is the mother goddess and the real power behind each one of the Trinity of Vishnu Ji, Brahma Ji and Shiv Ji. She takes the form of their wives, namely Lakshmi Ji, Saraswati Ji and Parvati Ji respectively. Without her support, they may not be complete. However, her most popular manifestation is that of Durga Ji.

ABODE
Always by the side of Vishnu Ji

IMPORTANCE
She is the Goddess of wealth & fortune. Newly wed bride is often called Lakshmi in the hope that she brings prosperity to the family.

SOME OTHER NAMES / EPITHETS
1. Shridevi
2. Bhudevi
3. Padma /Padmaja
4. Jaladhija
5. Chanchala
6. Lok Mata
7. Gajalakshmi
8. Rajya Lakshmi
9. Jayalakshmi
10. Grah Lakshmi
11. Bhagya Lakshmi
12. Yasholakshmi
13. Varalakshmi

TYPICAL DEPICTION
● On the left side of Vishnu Ji (See under depiction of Vishnu Ji)
● Standing or seated on lotus, flanked by an elephant on either side, holding garland on their raised trunks.
● She is decorated with jewellery and regal clothes, holding a white lotus in her hand and gold coins dropping from her hand.

SOME TEMPLES
● Appears alongside Vishnu Ji in all temples dedicated to Vishnu Ji

RELATED FESTIVALS / CEREMONIES
● Diwali, the festival of lights, is a time to especially worship Lakshmi Ji.
● *Lakshmi Pooja* is performed by traders at the beginning of their financial year as well as daily at the time of opening their shops/offices.
● Varalakshmi Pooja is performed by women in the South for blessings of long life for their husbands.

SOME INTERESTING INFORMATION
● Her vehicle is owl *(Ulooka)* used when travelling separately.
● Some scholars feel that it was only near the end of *Puranic period* (600 BC-200AD) that Lakshmi Ji got associated as Vishnu Ji's wife.
● Businessmen/traders worship her along with Ganesh Ji for unhindered financial prosperity. Images of both of them are kept in the premises and worshipped first thing when starting the day.
● Lakshmi Ji is known to have appeared as river Padmavati and also as sacred plant Tulsi.

BRAHMA JI
CREATOR OF THE UNIVERSE

Brahma Ji is not worshipped much because of a curse pronounced by Shiv Ji. Legend has it that once Brahma Ji was annoyed with Vishnu Ji when he addressed him as a small child whereas, Brahma Ji considered himself senior as creator of the universe. As a result, a fierce fight ensued between the two. Suddenly, a column of fire appeared, of which, neither end could be seen. Both of them agreed to investigate the terminal points of this wonderful column, one terminal point to be investigated by each. While Vishnu Ji set out in the form of a boar, Brahma Ji manifested himself in the form of a swan. Having failed to find the ends of the coloum, both returned. At this point in time, Shiv Ji appeared from the column, surrounded by several gods, causing relief to both Vishnu Ji and Brahma Ji. As a matter of ego, Brahma Ji falsely declared that he had seen one end of the column and, as voucher to his statement, displayed a flower of Ketaki which he had picked up from there. All this while, Vishnu Ji remained truthful about his failure to locate the other end of the column. Brahma Ji's falsehood infuriated Shiv Ji who cursed him that in future, Brahma Ji will not be worshipped. Shiv Ji also clarified that in the trinity of Brahma Ji -Vishnu Ji- Mahesh Ji (Shiv Ji's another name), each one was as important as the other, each one being equally significant for the existence, governance and protection of the universe. It may be interesting to note here that Ketaki flower is never offered in Shiv Ji's worship.

ORIGIN
Born from embryo which took shape in Vishnu Ji's mind when he began to think of creating universe and appeared on the lotus emanating from the navel of Vishnu Ji.
Brahma Ji has a definite age and gets dissolved into Vishnu Ji, to reappear repeatedly to create the universe anew in the rhythmic process of cosmic cycle

ABODE
Omnipresent, but his favoured abode is the fabled *Brahma-Lok*.

IMPORTANCE
Active creator of the universe. After destruction of one universe when another new universe is to be created, Brahma Ji appears on the lotus springing from the navel of Vishnu Ji and creates a New World, pronouncing *Om*. Such a new world remains in existence for one day of Brahama Ji (equivalent to about 4320 million man years).

Brahma Ji receives little attention during currency of a world because, having played his role, he goes to sleep and ceases to function actively. Brahma Ji is in any case, unpopular because he is known to be careless in granting boons to demons unguardedly, particularly to demons like *Hiranyakashipu* and *Ravan*, necessitating Vishnu Ji to intervene and appear in different incarnations to kill these demons. For this reason, Hindus began to think of Brahma Ji as the sole god of worship for demons.

SOME OTHER NAMES/EPITHETS
1. Prajapati
2. Kinjaja
3. Ashtakarna
4. Chaturnan/Chaturmukh
5. Nabhija

TYPICAL DEPICTION
Normally shown as having four heads & four arms holding lotus flower, spectre bow, string of beads, bowl & Vedas, dressed in white, having red skin. Usually shown old and bearded, riding his vehicle swan (hans) or squatting on lotus.

SOME TEMPLES
- Pushkar Lake Temple (Ajmer, Rajasthan)
- Temple in Dera (Kullu, HP)

RELATED FESTIVALS / CEREMONIES
Not worshipped much, except at the above temples specifically during *Baisakh & Sawan*. In many places in HP, devotees place a black stone under banyan trees and worship it as Brahma Ji's image.

SOME INTERESTING INFORMATION

Myth has it that originally Brahma Ji had only one head. From his body, he created a very beautiful woman Shatrupa, also called Saraswati. Brahma Ji fell in love with her and kept looking at her. She felt shy and started moving in different directions to escape Brahma Ji's gaze. For convenience sake, Brahma Ji, developed 5 heads, including one at top. The fifth head at top was later cut off by Shiv Ji, once when Brahma Ji talked disrespectfully to him.

●6 of the 18 Puraans are addressed to Brahma Ji.

●From the union of Brahma Ji & Shatrupa, came Manu, the progenitor of mankind.

●Brahma Ji's name should not be confused with Brahm, the supreme soul or the Absolute.

●Brahma Ji is credited with creation of demons from his thighs, gods from his mouth, sub-human species & other animates and inanimate from his sides and humans from his body.

●Brahma ji is the most obscure and outmoded god in the Hindu pantheon, inspite of being the first member of the most exhalted supreme trinity of Brahma-Vishnu-Mahesh(Shiv) and being the creator of the world . Cumulative effect of several negative deeds on part of Brahma Ji, including the one of his falsehood (described in the opening passage), his incest toward Shatrupa and more importantly, his wanton grant of boons to demons, resulted in cessation of his worship.

SARASWATI JI
GODDESS OF LEARNING & WIFE OF BRAHMA JI

Although generally taken as the wife of Brahma Ji, she is a river goddess according to the Vedas. Saraswati river, in the vedic period, flowed down from the Himalayas but is understood to have dried up and lost its existence due to a curse by sage Uthathya, to god of waters *Varun*, for abducting the wife of the sage.

ORIGIN
Saraswati Ji came into being from Brahma Ji's head (therefore called *Manas Kanya*) when he was meditating while trying to create the world.

ABODE
Alongwith Brahama Ji, she is eternal & omnipresent. She is also considered to reside in musical instruments and items used in learning (inkpot/pen etc.). She is also known to be sitting on the tongue of persons at the moment when any truthful statement comes from them, somewhat unintentionally.

IMPORTANCE
She is goddess of learning, knowledge and speech and is credited with the invention of *Devnagari* script as well as the invention of writing itself. She is also known as the river goddess, in the Vedas.

TYPICAL DEPICTION
Milky complexion, beautiful, sitting on lily and playing *Vina* (lute). Also shown riding swan or peacock, her vehicles.

SOME TEMPLES
Images of Saraswati Ji can be found in temples dedicated to other gods also.
Her sculptures exist in Halibid in Karnataka

showing her as dancing Saraswati Ji. As Sharda, she is worshipped in Maihar Temple situated on Trikoot Hill in M.P. Maihar is slang for Mai ka Haar (Garland of Devi) which fell on the hilltop.

RELATED FESTIVALS

She is worshipped in schools with morning prayers.
Basant Panchmi, when winter is over, is a special day for her worship.

OTHER INTERESTING INFORMATION

In the *Vedas*, Saraswati Ji is associated with river *Saraswati* but later recognised more as a goddess of knowledge encompassing all creative arts and one who bestows poets, artists, musicians etc.

She is understood to have cursed Lakshmi Ji to appear as a plant on earth. *Tulsi* is a result of this curse. In retaliation, Lakshmi Ji cursed her to appear on earth as a river which happened to be river Saraswati.

Myth has it that once when Brahma Ji was performing a religious ceremony and wanted his wife Saraswati Ji to be by his side, she did not come on time. Furious Brahma Ji told attend-

ing gods to fetch the first woman they see, for substituting Saraswati Ji. Gods went out and saw one milkmaid named *Gayatri*, brought her to Brahma Ji, who instantly married her and gave her Saraswati Ji's place and performed the ceremony. When Saraswati Ji finally turned up, she was very annoyed and cursed all present there as follows:-

Brahama Ji -You will not be worshipped

Vishnu Ji - You will be born as man on earth and suffer separation from your wife (later incarnated as Ram Chandr Ji)

Shiv Ji -You will be deprived of manhood

Indr -You will lose your divine kingdom

Agni -You will have to recklessly consume everything whether good or bad.

Brahmans (priests) -You will be confined to perform poojas only, depending on food offered by devotees.

Lakshmi Ji -You will remain with sinners.

Other goddesses -None of you will bear children

However, Gayatri Ji took this opportunity to marginally modify Saraswati Ji's curse, to the benefit of all those cursed.

Actually this milkmaid was none other than personification of *Gayatri,* the *Vedic* hymn.

● According to Hindu scriptures, Saraswati ji is among the five goddess which emerged (along with Parvati Ji, Lakshmi Ji, Savitri Ji & Radha Ji)

from the supreme spirit, endowed with the force of learning.

● According to earlier mythology, Saraswati Ji was one of the wives of Vishnu ji, alongwith Laxmi Ji & Ganga Ji. Once Saraswati Ji got jealous of sharing Vishnu Ji with the other two and cursed Lakshmi Ji to become plant Tulsi and Ganga Ji to become a river on earth where people would wash off their sins. In retaliation, Ganga ji also cursed Saraswati Ji to become a river to flow in the nether world.

SHIV JI
DESTROYER OF EVIL

Shiv Ji is associated with snakes (round his neck) and tiger skin (as his *aasan*). According to one legend, once Shiv Ji, accompanied by Vishnu Ji in the guise of a beautiful woman, appeared to subdue a group of hermits who were against religious orthodoxy. To counter this, the hermits unleased a fierce tiger and set it against Shiv Ji, who killed it and took its skin, to use it later as his *aasan*. Next, the hermits released a cobra to attack Shiv Ji, who tamed it also and placed it round his neck. Lastly, the hermits sent out a fierce dwarf to attack Shiv Ji, who put it under his feet and started performing a brilliant dance. After all this, the hermits acknowledged Shiv Ji as *Pashupati*, the master of animals. It may be noted that this also symbolises Shiv Ji's control on animal instincts in humans.

ORIGIN
Sprang from the forehead of Brahma Ji.

ABODE
He is also omnipresent but his favoured place is *Mount Kailash* located in the Himalayas. Other places frequented by him include Kashi and *Triumbakeshwar* located in Uttranchal and Maharashtra respectively. Shiv Ji is one among the holy trinity. He represents generation, destruction and regeneration. Origin of the practice of yog is credited to him.

SOME OTHER NAMES/ EPITHET

Ardhnarishwar	Trinetra
Adinath	Trinayana
Bhambhru	Mrityunjaya
Bhima	Tapakeshwar
Bhairon	Tribhunvan
Ekambereshwar	Mahadev
Gangadhar	Neelkanth
Kailashpati	Vishwanath
Ishan	Natraj
Shankar	Vaidyanath
Jatadhar	Pashupati
Shambhu	Yogiraj
Sarva	Rudra
Sadashiv	Yogeshwar
Mahesh	Mahakal

TYPICAL DEPICTION
Sitting on a tiger skin, cobras around neck, long hair tied into a mop atop head, crescent on the mop of hair (acquired during samudra manthan), *Ganga* falling from above on to his head and then flowing down, holding trident, ash smeared all over his body, holding mendicant's bowl. Accompanying him usually, are his wife Parvati Ji, son Ganesh Ji and his vehicle bull, named *Nandi*.
● A drum (damru) is also shown with him, either in his hand or affixed to his trident.
● A third eye on the forehead, which when opened, can destroy anything, even the whole universe.
● Represented as *Shivling*, symbolising his generative power.

SOME TEMPLES
- *Chidambaram* Temple (TN)
- 12 *Jyotrilings* said to be of divine origin (*Somnath* in Gujarat, *Mallikarjun* in AP, *Mahakaleshwar* in MP, *Omkar eshwar* at the confluence of river *Narmada & Kaveri* i n M.P, *Kedarnath* in Uttaranchal, *Bhima Shankar* in Mahararshtra, *Kashi Vishvanath* in Varanasi U.P., *Triumbakeshwar & Vaidyanath* in Mahararshtra, *Naganath* in Gujarat, *Rameshwaram* in TN and *Ghrishneshwar* in Maharashtra)
- *Tapakeshwar* Temple in Dehra Dun, Uttranchal
- *Amarnath* in Kashmir

RELATED FESTIVALS/ CEREMONIES
Shivratri in the month of *Magh* is in respect of Shiv Ji. It is based on a legend about a hunter who was sleeping on a tree when leaves kept falling below on a *Shivling*, as the hunter kept adjusting his position. Shiv Ji was very pleased and bestowed the hunter with good luck. This legend gave rise to celebrate *Shivratri*, when throughout the night, worshippers keep showering leaves on Shiv Ji's image.

Mondays are observed as day of fasting by Shiv Ji's devotees to please him.

OTHER INTERESTING INFORMATION
Ganga was brought from heaven by sage *Bhagirath* and as earth would not be able to bear the impact, it was received by Shiv Ji on his head and subsequently released to flow on earth.

During *samudra manthan*, ocean threw up poison, which could destroy all living beings. All the gods kept back except Shiv Ji who happily drank the poison to save others. While Shiv Ji was drinking this poison, Parvati Ji got alarmed and in an effort to prevent harm to Shiv Ji, she tried to hold Shiv Ji's throat. As a result, poison got stuck in Shiv Ji's throat rendering a blue tinge. For this blue tinge in his neck, he is named *Neelkanth*.

As *Natraj*, he is said to have created the basis for dancing. To destroy the world at the end of each cosmic cycle, he performs a deadly dance called *Tandav Nritya*.

Shiv Ji cut off Brahma Ji's one head in a quarrel. Feeling very bad about it, Shiv Ji retired to Kashi (Varanasi), living as an ascetic and surviving on alms. Parvati Ji, as *Annapurna*, followed him there so that he gets food properly. This great service of Paravti Ji so impressed Shiv Ji that out of love, he hugged Paravti Ji so intensely that both of them got merged, giving rise to the form of *Ardhnarishwar*, half-man half-woman.

- Shiv Ji is associated with the phrase, *Satyam Shivam Sundaram* meaning truth, supremacy and beauty. Literally, in *Sanskrit*, Shiv means good and auspicious.
- Marriage between Shiv Ji and Sati can be called the first love marriage in this world.

After the death of his first wife Sati, Shiv Ji was very annoyed and kept travelling all over the world with the dead body of Sati. To bring normalcy, Vishnu Ji used his *Sudershan Chakra* to cut off the body of Sati in order to disperse it. These cut off limbs fell at different places which became sacred spots, later called *Shaktipiths*. Shiv Ji is understood to guard each of these spots in the form of *Bhairav*.

- 6 of the 18 *Puraans* are addressed to Shiv Ji

PARVATI JI
GODDESS OF FERTILITY & WIFE OF SHIV JI

In her form as Durga Ji, she is adored most. In fact most of the goddesses including Lakshmi Ji and Saraswati Ji, are believed to be manifestations of this goddess, who is considered as the ultimate source of all the powers which energise Vishnu Ji, Brahma Ji & Shiv Ji and hence also called Maa Shakti. Unless inspired by this shakti (power), Vishnu Ji can not act as the preserver of the universe, Brahma Ji can not cause creation of the universe and Shiv Ji can not do his task of destruction.

ORIGIN

Parvati Ji is daughter of king Himalaya. Earlier she was born as *Sati*, daughter of King Daksha, (one of the ancestors of mankind and originator of *Sanatan Dharm)* but sacrificed herself on the fire, being unable to bear insult of husband Shiv Ji

ABODE

Alongwith Shiv Ji at *Mount Kailash*

IMPORTANCE

She is the most revered goddess among Hindus and is identified as the greatest goddess Devi, wife of Shiv Ji and mother of Ganesh Ji and Kartikeya Ji. In her mild form, she is Paravati Ji, while in her fierce form, she is Durga who assumed nine other forms to kill demons Mahishasur, Shumbh, Nishumbh etc. who had displaced gods from heaven.

As *Annapurana Ji* she is worshipped as goddess of fertility and abundance, with particular reference to food. Parvati Ji is worshipped by young girls to become successful wives like Parvati Ji.

SOME OTHER NAMES/ EPITHETS

Like Shiv Ji, she also has 1008 names. Some very popular names are:

Ambika	Kalyani
Kali	Shitala
Shyama	Chandi
Bhawani	Mahamaya
Tripurasundari	Uma
Durga	Jagdamba
Mansa	Sheranwali
Gauri	Naina
Jwala	
Rati	

TYPICAL DEPICTION

As Parvati Ji, she is golden faced, wears silky white dress and carries no weapons.

As Durga Ji, she sits on a lion, has ten arms, one arm holding long pointed spear or trident, shown killing demon *Mahishasur*. As *Kali*, she is black and terrifying but herself, she is fearless. She is the killer of demon Raktabeej, drinking his blood before it can touch ground (since otherwise more *Raktabeejs* would sprout from ground). After killing *Raktabeej*, she is shown dancing in ecstasy, causing earth to shake. To control this, Shiv Ji lays himself on ground in front of Kali, who steps on him, gets embarrassed, her tongue protrudes out and the dreadful dance comes to a halt.

RELATED FESTIVALS/ CEREMONIES

Durga Pooja or *Navratri* in the month of a *Ashwin* (more popularly celebrated in Bengal) celebrating return of Parvati Ji to her father's home to stay for 9 days. On the 10th day, she is given farewell by immersing her image in waters, signifying her return to *Mount Kailash.*

● *Navratri* is observed twice a year (Oct/Nov & Mar/Apr). It is said that Ram Chandr Ji wanted to pray

Durga Ji for help in his fight against the ten headed demon Ravan but could not wait till Oct/Nov, the conventional time for *Durga Pooja* and therefore, prayed her at that very time (Mar/Apr) when he was proceeding to *Lanka* to kill *Ravan*. Thus started the custom of observing *Durga Pooja* twice a year.

● *Gangaur* is observed as a day of fasting by young girls to become good housewives like Paravati Ji herself.

● *Annakoot* festival (more particularly celebrated in Brijbhoomi and Varanasi) is in honour of Paravati Ji's appearance as Annapurna Devi to assist Shiv Ji during his days in Varanasi.

SOME TEMPLES

There are several temples where Parvati Ji's idol is placed alongwith Shiv Ji.

There are also many temples exclusively for Durga Ji, in many parts of the country.

●Temples at Kalka Ji and Jhandewalan in New Delhi & Vaishnav Devi Ji in J&K, are very popular.

●Shitala Mata temple in Amritsar.

●Annapurna temples in Varanasi.

OTHER INTERESTING/ INFORMATION

Association of Shiv Ji with *Sati* and Parvati Ji can be described in following sequence:

When Shiv Ji did not permit his wife Sati to visit her father's house during a special religious ceremony, she got furious and to demonstrate her superiority, she disclosed her several forms including the soft one like Gauri and more importantly her fierce form of Durga. After this demonstration, Shiv Ji realised her true powers and agreed to let her go. When she arrived at her father's place, she felt insulted by the fact that her father considered her husband Shiv Ji as an unwelcome ascetic and jumped into the ceremonial fire. Sati's death caused Shiv Ji great grief. He took her body in his arms and wandered all over the world in anger, causing great turmoil. Gods requested Vishnu Ji to calm down Shiv Ji. Vishnu Ji fired his *Sudarshan Chakra* on Sati's body (or with arrows). Spots where parts of her body fell, become holy spots and world was saved from destruction. But Shiv Ji took up life of an ascetic. Sati was reborn to Himmavat as Parvati who was very serious about marrying Shiv Ji, much against the advice of her father. Parvati came to Shiv Ji's side, fasted and did prayers, ultimately pleasing Shiv Ji and they were then married.

Apart from Parvati Ji's manifestation as Durga Ji with the beautiful face to lure demons, she assumed nine fierce forms to kill demons. These, according to one of the several descriptions available, can be briefly described as follows.

●**Dash-Bhuja**: Having ten arms, each arm carrying a different weapon, to destroy a part of the demon army.

●**Sinh-Vahini**: Riding lion, to fight demon Rakta Beej who had the power of springing up many demons from each drop of his blood falling on the ground.

●**Mahishasur-Mardini**: Killer of demon Mahishasur when he appeared in the form of a buffalo.

●**Jagatdhatri**: Another manifestation to kill an army of demons

●**Kali**: As dark complexioned, to drink the blood of demon Rakta Beej while fighting him to ensure that his blood does not reach the ground, which would otherwise cause springing up of more demons.

●**Muktakeshi**: With flowing hair, she killed another army of demons.

●**Tara**: The manifestation in which she killed demon Shumbh

●**Chhinamatika**: To kill demon Nishumbh.

●**Jagadgauri**: The manifestations in which Durga Ji was worshipped by all the gods, for their salvation from demons.

GANESH JI

GOD OF AUSPICIOUS BEGINNINGS & REMOVER OF OBSTACLES

One evening, Vishnu Ji appeared as a priest in front of Shiv Ji & Parvati Ji and requested them to let him be their son. Bemused, they gave their consent. The priest (Vishnu Ji) then transformed himself into a beautiful child', to the delight of the new-found parents. On this happy occasion, all the gods came over to bless the new child. Vishnu Ji (himself) blessed him as a repository of knowledge, Brahma Ji blessed him with fame and to be the foremost god for worship & Lakshmi Ji blessed that she will dwell wherever this child is adored. Similarly other gods & goddesses also blessed him with other qualities. This is the origin of Ganesh Ji.

ORIGIN

According to another legend, Ganesh Ji was produced from the sweat of Parvati Ji who deputed him to guard the place when she wanted privacy while having a bath. When Shiv Ji arrived, Ganesh Ji did not allow him in, as he was unaware of the identity of Shiv Ji. This enraged Shiv Ji who cut off Ganesh Ji's head. When Parvati Ji discovered this and explained the truth to Shiv Ji, he felt sorry. Shiv Ji then ordered his attendants to bring head of any baby whose mother may be asleep. Attendants saw a baby elephant in such a position and brought its head which was then transplanted by Shiv Ji on Ganesh Ji's body. To further console Parvati Ji, who was still in tears seeing an elephants head on her son's body, Brahma Ji announced that Ganesh Ji will have precedence over other gods in the matter of worship.

ABODE

Eternal and omnipresent, he is generally at Mount Kailash, along with parents Shiv Ji and Parvati Ji

IMPORTANCE

Ganesh Ji is the god of auspicious beginnings. Major

religious and other activities commence with the phrase 'Om Shri Ganeshay Namah' meaning we pray to Ganesh Ji. He is worshipped to invoke his blessing to surmount all difficulties and ensure success in any venture.

Ganesh Ji is given pre-eminence over other gods as granted by Brahma Ji. In addition to what has been mentioned above, legend has it that once there was a competition amongst gods for the first place of worship. It was decided that the god who traverses the universe fastest will be declared winner. All the gods and goddesses began the race on their fastest vehicles whereas Ganesh Ji, with his limitations of pot belly and slow moving vehicle mouse, took a round of parents Shiv Ji and Parvati Ji and then sat down. He was declared winner since parents are considered to be universe in themselves. Since then Ganesh Ji is treated & worshipped as first among gods.

SOME OTHER NAMES /EPITHETS

1. Ekdant
2. Lambakarna
3. Modakpriya
4. Ganapati
5. Lambodara
6. Vighneshwar
7. Gajanan
8. Vinayak
9. Gajadhipati

TYPICAL DEPICTION

Ganesh Ji has elephant's head and four arms, holding shell, discus, club and lily. Has serpent around his waist and his vehicle mouse alongside.

● Always shown with a tray of sweets (modak) and having pot belly.

● In some images, he is shown holding sugarcane bow.

● Ganesh Ji is sometimes shown in playfully dancing pose.

● To signify his association with knowledge and prosperity, sometimes Ganesh Ji is depicted seated alongwith Lakshmi Ji and Saraswati Ji.

SOME TEMPLES

In all temples of Shiv Ji & Paravati Ji, he is shown alongside.

His idol is usually placed at the entrance of temples, in line with the myth about his guarding the entrance to Paravati Ji's private chamber.

● Siddhi Vinayak Temple, Mumbai (Maharashtra)

● Ganesh Dhundiraja Temple, Varanasi (UP)

● Ashth Vinayak Temples 8 temples near Pune in (Maharashtra)

● Rajangaoncha Mahaganpati Temple, Rajangaon (Maharashtra)

●Chintamani Vinayak Temple, Theur (Maharashtra)

RELATED FESTIVALS / CEREMONIES

Ganpati Mahotsav is held sometime around August, more popularly in Maharashtra, when Ganesh Ji idols are installed in every locality, worshipped for ten days and finally immersed in sea/river.

SOME INTERESTING INFORMATION

●His vehicle mouse symbolises capability to destroy every obstacle.

●When Parshuram (an incarnation of Vishnu Ji) came to visit Shiv Ji on Mount Kailash, Shiv Ji was sleeping. Ganesh Ji, who was guarding the entrance refused entry to him. At this Parshuram got enraged and threw his axe (a gift from Shiv Ji to him) to attack Ganesh Ji. Realising it as the sacred thing originally belonging to his father, Ganesh Ji received it, with humility, on his tusks, one of which got severed off partially. Thereafter, Ganesh Ji is also called Ekdant.

●Ganesh Ji is said to have two wives, *Siddhi* (Success) & *Riddhi* (Prosperity). It is therefore presumed that whoever worships Ganesh Ji and pleases him, gains success and prosperity.

●His elder brother is Kartikeya Ji.

●In Kerala, Ganesh Ji's image is covered with a sweet preparation in honour of Ganesh Ji's liking for sweets.

●*Swastik* is known to be graphic symbolisation of Ganesh Ji.

KARTIKEYA JI
GOD OF WAR

According to Hindu mythology, Kartikeya Ji resides on the *Krauncha Mount* in the south, hence more popular and worshipped there, than in the northern parts of India. Ditto with the festivals related to Kartikeya Ji, such as *Skand Shasthi*, as well as with the temples devoted to him.

ORIGIN
The elder of the two sons of Shiv Ji & Parvati Ji. Krithikas, wives of six sages acted individually as surrogate mothers with the seed of Shiv Ji, delivering six boys. At birth, these boys were thrown off together, by these surrogate mothers. Lying in the forest, these six boys merged into one and became Karthikeya.

ABODE
Mount Kailash, alongwith Shiv Ji, Parvati Ji & Ganesh Ji.
Also *Krauncha Mount* in the South (after his tiff with his parents over their being more favourable to Ganesh Ji, he left and went to *Mount Krauncha*).

IMPORTANCE
He was born with the clear objective of slaying one demon *Tarak* who was causing great disturbance in the gods' domain by way of disturbing the rhythm in seasons. Kartikeya Ji was, for this reason, appointed as Commander - in-Chief of the devine forces.

Kartikeya Ji had more of destructive inclination, being born out of Shiv Ji's seed as compared to Ganesh Ji who was born out of Parvati Ji's sweat.

SOME OTHER NAMES/ EPITHETS
1. Shadanan
2. Subramanyam
3. Tarakajit
4. Skand
5. Agnibhoo
6. Kumar
7. Murugan
8. Gangaputra
9. Senapati
10. Nayak

TYPICAL DEPICTION
Kartikeya Ji is generally depicted as very handsome, bright complexioned and holding spear, arrow, sword, discus, noose, shield & conch in one hand and the other hand in a gesture of blessing.

Rides a peacock, which was also his vehicle during fight against demon *Tarak*.

Also shown as a guardian deity in Shiv Ji's temples.

SOME TEMPLES
Shree Mallikarjun, Srisailam (known as Mount Kailash of South India) in T.N.
Shaila Mount in A.P.
Kapaleshwar Temple, T.N.
Chidambaram Temple, T.N.
Murugan Temple, T.N.

RELATED FESTIVALS
Skand Shasthi celebrated in South as

the day on which Kartikeya Ji defeated demon *Tarak*.

Kartikeya Ji is also worshipped alongwith Durga Ji in Bengal.

OTHER INTERESTING INFORMATION
Since Kartikeya Ji was born through surrogate mothers under a secret plan of stealth by gods, depriving, Parvati Ji of the pleasure of motherhood, Parvati Ji cursed all divine females (goddesses) that none will ever be capable of producing a child. Kartikeya's wife's is Devasena.

VISHNU JI'S INCARNATIONS
INCLUDING RAM CHANDR JI & KRISHN JI

It was the curse of sages *Shukra* and *Bhrigu* that Vishnu Ji was condemned to be born several times on earth. This curse coincided with Vishnu Ji's powers to preserve, restore and protect his devotees to whom he had promised that he will incarnate himself whenever evil overwhelms and demons make life unbearable. He appears on earth, to restore order and righteousness.

Popularly, a ten-incarnation myth is well accepted. However, the myth varies in different *Puraans*, some claming it to be 22 or even more.

It is worth mentioning here that Krishn Ji, the 8th incarnation, is understood to be a complete and ideal *avataar* of Vishnu Ji, while all other incarnations appeared for limited/specific purpose only.

1ST INCARNATION
MATSYA, THE FISH

Appeared during *Satyug* (also known as *Krityug*) the period of truth & purity, to take out Vedas from the ocean to enable Brahma Ji work on the cyclic process of creation of universe. One school of thought propounds it as an incarnation to save *Manu*, the first of mankind on earth, during the great floods (*pralay*) which destroyed everything pertaining to the previous universe.

2ND INCARNATION
KURMA, THE TORTOISE

Appeared during Satyug, to hold on his back, the newly created globe and help it to stabilise itself. Another myth, not much different, has it that when powers of gods waned due to a curse by sage Durvasa, they approached Vishnu Ji to save them from evils of demons and help them achieve eternity. Vishnu Ji advised them to jointly churn the ocean with demons, using Mount Mandara as churning rod and the giant snake Vasuki as the rope. The mountain being too heavy began to sink. At this stage Vishnu Ji appeared as the gigantic tortoise Kurma, to bear the mountain on his back which facilitated the process of churning of the ocean - *Samudra Manthan*

3RD INCARNATION
VARAHA, THE BOAR

Appeared near end of Satyug, to save earth during world destruction caused by demon king Hiranyakash, elder son of sage Kashyap. He rescued the earth out from deep waters by taking it on his tusks and at the same time killing the demon.

4TH INCARNATION
NARASHIMHA, HALF-MAN HALF-LON

Appeared at the end of *Satyug*, to save his devotee Prahlad, son of cruel demon king Hiranyakashipu who was blessed against death (conditions applied) by Brahma Ji. Narasimha killed the demon, ensuring that the special conditions under the boon were honoured - such as "he can't be killed either by a man or by an animal" -hence Vishnu Ji appeared as half-man half-lion. There were some other similar conditions which were also taken care of.

5TH INCARNATION
VAMAN, THE DWARF

Appeared during Satyug as son of sage Kashyap and his wife Aditi to restore heaven to gods, from Bali, a demon king and grandson of Prahlad. Bali had earlier defeated gods and captured their heaven. Gods requested Vishnu Ji for help. At this, Vishnu Ji took the form of a dwarf and appeared before king Bali at a time when he was conducting a religious ceremony and giving away gifts to Brahmans. Bali asked this Brahman in diminutive form to ask for anything. At this Vaman asked for as much land as he could measure in three steps. Bali agreed but to his utter surprise, Vaman covered heaven in his first step and earth in the second step. As a consideration for Bali's kindness, Vaman left Patal, the nether world to Bali. It may be interesting to note that the festival of *Onam*, celebrated in Kerala, is linked to this

6TH INCARNATION
PARSHURAM, THE BRAHMAN

Appeared at close of Satyug, to repress tyranny of powerful Kshatriyas. He was born to hermit Jamdagini and his wife Renuka. The sixth & the seventh incarnations of Vishnu Ji existed simultaneously. Parshuram confronted Ram Chandr Ji immediately after he broke the divine bow in the court of King Janak to marry his daughter Sita Ji. Parshuram was a hot headed person who would easily pick up fights such as with Ganesh Ji & Ram Chandr Ji. Lakshmi Ji incarnated herself as his wife Dharini.

7TH INCARNATION
RAM CHANDR JI,
THE RIGHTEOUS

Appeared at the end of Tretayug, the second age of the world, to give lessons in righteousness and killing the ten-headed demon king of Lanka, Ravan. He also curtailed Parshuram's ambitions against Kshatriyas.

Lakshmi Ji incarnated herself as Sita Ji, his wife. Ram Chandr Ji is also known by other names such as Ragahav, Purushottam etc. The whole story of Ram Chandr Ji is to demonstrate the value of systems of Hindu Society- as scripted in the epic Ramayan by sage Valmiki. and at the same time killing the demon.

8TH INCARNATION
KRISHN JI THE ORATOR OF
GITA ON THE SIGNIFICANCE
OF *KARM* (DUTY)

Appeared in Duaparyug. This avataar also appeared to kill evil doers and more importantly to lead Pandavs in the war against their cousins Kauravs, the war known as Mahabharat.

Lakshmi Ji also incarnated herself as his wife Rukmini. Some other names given to Krishn Ji include Banke Behari, Gopal, Murari, Ghanshyam etc. The tale around Krishn Ji i.e. Mahabharat, including Gita, was scripted by sage Vyas.

9TH INCARNATION
BUDDH , THE RELIGIOUS TEACHER

Lived during 563-483 BC and founded Buddhism, a mix of several ancient teachings and systems, relatively unorthodox as compared to vedic traditions. His teachings were more or less *Upanishads* put into action. However his teachings which were focussed on non-violence, did some damage, as people became more docile and susceptible to attacks of outsiders. It may be worthwhile to mention here that while all the incarnations of Vishnu Ji are mythical, this 9th incarnation as Buddh is based on recorded history. Lakshmi Ji also appeared with him as a monk. According to a different school of thought, Balram, the powerful brother of Krishn Ji was an incarnation of Vishnu Ji and not Buddh. Krishn Ji is then sequenced younger as the 9th incarnation and Balram the 8th.

10TH INCARNATION
KALKI

Schduled to appear sometime in future, at the end of *Kalyug,* an era or yug which began around the times of Mahabharat war. This incarnation of Vishnu Ji would be to restore purity in the world and the cycle of the yugs to restart with Satyug again. Kalki incarnation is propounded to appear riding a horse and holding a sword. Since this incarnation is yet to appear and, as clear details are unavailable, he is not worshipped.

OTHER POPULAR GODS, GODDESSES, DEITIES AND MYTHLOGICAL EVENTS

Airawat

The King of elephants. Emerged during Samudra Manthan. It is the mount of god Indr.

Agni Dev

The Vedic god of fire. Instrumental in establishing contact between worshipped and the worshipper, carries man's offerings to gods as it rises from earth towards heaven. Son of Brahma Ji, he brings gods to the altar of worship and is invoked as a witness in all Hindu rituals like havan, marriage etc. Agni Pariksha (ordeal by fire) is considered an ultimate test to prove truth or purity of a person.

Ardhnarishwar

Half-man Half -woman image of Shiv Ji & Parvati Ji (read under Annapurna devi).

Annapurna Devi

Goddess of plenty of grains, a benevolent form of Parvati Ji. Worshipped alongwith Shiv Ji & Parvati Ji in many temples since she is understood to be an incarnation of Parvati Ji when she followed Shiv Ji, (to serve him) who was wandering as a mendicant, repenting the killing of a Brahman by him. By her service, Annapurna Devi pleased Shiv Ji so much that he embraced her so fiercely that they both merged to form a single personality of Ardhnarishwar.

Brahaspati

Counsellor of gods and their high priest. He is ruler of planet Jupiter and week's 4th day Thursday is named after him.

Chitragupt Ji

The record keeper in heaven for deeds of persons to facilitate decision about sending him /her to heaven or hell, after death. He is understood to have come into existence from Brahma Ji's mind when he was meditating. He was hiding in Brahma Ji's body. He is known to be progenitor of Kayasth clan, predominantly in the North.

Dhanvantri

Physician of gods and originator of Ayurveda, the Indian science of medicine. He appeared during Samudra Manthan, carrying vessel filled with medicines and amrit

Ganga

The goddess representing holy river Ganga. According to legend, goddess Ganga was produced from the sweat of Vishnu Ji's feet which Brahma Ji collected in his Kamandal (water container) and later released it to fall on earth. To avoid disaster from the impact of its fall, Shiv Ji received her on his matted hair and subsequently released it on earth. Ganga is considered very holy and a bath in its water absolves the bather of sins and opens doors of heaven for him. Ganga water is considered very sacred by Hindus. With this water in his palm, a Hindu is not expected to say any untruth. Also Ganga water remains so good & pure permanently, it does not deteriorate on keeping for any period of time.

Garud

The vehicle of Vishnu Ji and the bird god. He is said to have released Ram Chandr Ji and his brother Lakshman from snake bind (Nagpash) during their fight against Ravan. His son Jatayu was also involved in fighting Ravan when he was running away after abducting Sita Ji.

Hanuman Ji

The monkey god who helped Ram Chandra Ji during his fight against Ravan and is therefore considered as god of power & strength. He is worshipped in temples all over the country. Tuesdays are special days for his worship. In the tale of Ramayan, following incidents are specially relevant to Hanuman Ji.

● Crossing the sea in one leap to reach Ashok Vatika, the garden in the Kingdom of Ravan where Sita Ji was confined. There he gave her the message about arrival of Ram Chandr Ji to rescue her.

● Bringing a whole mountain for one herb (Sanjivni) to revive Lakshman from unconsciousness during a battle.

● Burning Lanka with the fire put on his tail by Ravan's men.

This Monkey god is considered so holy that one can see lots of monkeys in Hindu temples and no one wishes to do the sin of harming a monkey. Hanuman has been blessed with immortality by Brahma Ji as well as by Ram Chandr Ji.

Hanuman Ji is also called Maruti & Pawan Putr. He is considered antidote to possible ill effects of Shani Dev.

Indr Dev

A Vedic god, chief among smaller gods and King of Amaravati (heaven). Lots of interesting mythological tales are associated with the rise and fall of Indr. He is also considered as the rain god and worshipped specially in case of draughts.

In post Vedic era, his stature got lowered as also his character. Myth has it that he tried to seduce Ahilya, wife of sage Gautam, who cursed Indra's downfall and Ahalya to become a rock, to be reinstated as a female, later by Ram Chandr Ji during his exile days in the forests.

Another myth has it that Indr was slighted by Krishn Ji by asking people not to worship Indr. As a revenge, Indr caused heavy downpour on Brijbhoomi (in U.P. around Mathura) but Krishn Ji took Goverdhan mountain up on his finger, under which all the people of Brijbhoomi were protected from the heavy downpour. Indr then recognised Krishn Ji's supremacy.

Jagannath

A special form of Krishn Ji without hands and legs. Main temple of Jagannath is in Puri (Orissa) where, also installed are images of his brother Balram and sister Subhadra. Jagannath literally means Lord of the Universe.

According to a legend, there was a king named Indradyuman who prayed to Vishnu Ji for his own salvation. Vishnu Ji told him to raise image of Jagannath and put into its belly, the remains of Krishn Ji. It may be noted that Krishn Ji was earlier killed by a hunter and, some people had put the remains of his body into a box. To help king Indradyuman, Vishnu Ji deputed Vishwakarma, the celestial architect, to make the image of Jagannath. Vishwakarma agreed to do so on the condition that while on the job, he should not be disturbed at all. After some days, the king's curiosity overtook him and he peeped into the workshop when Vishwakarma was working on the images. This annoyed Vishwakarma greatly and he left the job incomplete, that is images without hands and feet which were yet to be made. The king felt ashamed and sought Bramha Ji's help. Brahma Ji assured the King that the images would become famous for times to come and he himself would come and act as priest for installation. Although an yearly festival, every 12 years, as tradition now, these images are replaced with new ones as the old ones are buried. Snan (bath) Yatra and Rathyatra are conducted when these images are taken out, given bath with Ganga water and later taken out in procession. Devotees throw themselves under the wheels of the chariots carrying these idols.

This is one of the most popular festivals, held in the month of Ashadh (June-July) in several parts of the country.

It is interesting to note that the English word JUGGERNAUT originates from Krishn Ji's this name Jagannath and is attributed to institutions / concept to which persons blindly sacrifice themselves. Later the word juggernaut also came to mean person in a particular field who is extremely accomplished- a guru.

Kamdhenu

Also called Surabhi, the celestial cow of plenty which emerged during Samudra Manthan. It is believed that Brahma Ji created Vedas for Brahamans to recite and Kamdhenu cow to provide ghee (Hydroginated oil of natural origin) for burning sacrificial items during sacred ceremonies likes havan etc. For this reason, cows are highly revered by Hindus who call her 'Gaumata' - mother cow.

Kuber

The god of money. He is devotee of Shiv Ji and king of Yakshas, the spirits that reside in secluded forests supposedly guarding hidden treasures.

Nandi

The sacred bull and vehicle of Shiv Ji

Surya Dev

The sun god is one of the three most important Vedic gods, later superseded by the trinity of Brahma Ji, Vishnu Ji and Shiv Ji.

The vedic hymn Gayatri Mantra1 is in honour of Surya Dev. He is worshipped by Hindus by way of offering water to him at sunrise. A dynasty of powerful rulers called themselves Suryavanshi, being descendants of Surya Dev. Ram

Chandr Ji was the 66th king in this dynasty. Some other notable descendants of Surya Dev are Manu (progenitor of mankind and author of Dharm Shastra, the first book on law to guide and govern mankind), Yam (god of death), river Yamuna, Sugriv (who with his monkey army, assisted Ram Chandr Ji in his fight against Ravan), & Karn of Mahabharat (born illegitimately to Pandava's mother Kunti).

Solar eclipse (like lunar eclipse) has an interesting myth attached to it. During Samudra Manthan, when Vishnu Ji was deceitfully (appearing as beautiful dancer Mohini) distributing amrit (nectar/ ambrosia) only to gods, one demon got suspicious and mingled with gods and got a share of amrit. Surya Dev & Chandra Dev saw this and brought this to Vishnu Ji's (or Mohini's) attention. At this point, Vishnu Ji threw his Sundershan Chakra at this demon and cut him into two. Since he had consumed amrit he would not die and thus, his two parts, head part named Rahu and lower part called Ketu continue to live. The demon's animosity is reflected as solar eclipse when Ketu tries to swallow Sun and as lunar eclipse when Rahu tries to swallow Moon.

Narad

The celestial seer (rishi) as the messenger between gods but also responsible for making divine missions. His origin is from the head of Brahma Ji. An interesting tale about Narad is that once through his determination, he defeated the god of lust Kamdev. This caused great pride in himself. To teach Narad a lesson in humility, Vishnu Ji designed an act. He created an illusionary kingdom with a very beautiful Princess due to be married. Narad fell for her and requested Vishnu Ji for help by way of giving him (Narad) the most beautiful face and personality. Instead Vishnu Ji gave him the face of a monkey. Obviously, Narad was rejected by the Princess who, instead selected Vishnu Ji who had also appeared there as a suitor. Realising the trick played on him, Narad cursed Vishnu Ji that in one of his incarnations, he will suffer separation from his beloved wife and only a monkey will come to his rescue. Thus happened the tale of Ramayan, abduction of his wife Sita Ji by demon king Ravan and finally, the monkey god Hanuman coming to their rescue.

Narad's depiction is very typical, shown as a seer with long pointed tuft of hair, veena in one hand and always wandering. His name is associated with any person who indulges in unnecessary mischief by way of communication gap.

Samudra Manthan

Churning of the ocean by gods and demons to extract amrit (nectar/ambrosia) to achieve immortality. Legend has it that as powers of gods waned due to a curse by sage Durvasa, they approached Brahma Ji for guidance. He advised them to seek Vishnu Ji's help who, in turn, advised them to churn the ocean jointly with demons to extract amrit, using mount Mandara as the churning rod and the giant snake Vasuki as the rope. Vishnu Ji would himself incarnate as the giant tortoise Kurma (read under Vishnu Ji's incarnations for details) and hold the mountain on his back.

Churning of the ocean resulted in extraction/appearance of things as listed below (not necessarily in original sequence).

1. **Surabhi**-The devine cow claimed by gods (also called Kamdhenu)
2. **Varuni**-The goddess of wine.
3. **Parijaat**-The celestial Tree taken by Indr Dev and transplanted in Amaravati.
4. **Rambha**-The celestial dancer (Apsara).
5. **Chandra**-The cool moon taken by Shiv Ji for adornment on his head.
6. **Vish**-The poison consumed by Shiv Ji.
7. **Kastubha**-The precious stone claimed by Vishnu Ji
8. **Airawat**-The elephant with wings, taken by Indr Dev as his vehicle.
9. **Uchchaisravas**-The white horse having black tail, claimed by famous demon king Bali.
10. **Panchjanya**-The conch (shankh) taken by Vishnu Ji.
11. **Lakshmi Ji**-The goddess of wealth, taken by Vishnu Ji as his wife.
12. **Saranga**-The bow, taken by Vishnu Ji.
13. **Kaumodaki**-The mace (gada), also taken by Vishnu Ji.
14. **Dhanvantri**-The physician god, holding jar of medicines and amrit (nectar/ambrosia).

As the gods and demons started quarreling over the possession of amrit, Vishnu Ji appeared as a beautiful apsara Mohini to lure away demons and deceitfully distribute amrit only among the gods.

Shani Dev

The god of evil, also known as Kroor Drishti (evil look). Evil happenings are attributed to this god. To appease him and prevent any harm, people pay obeisance to this god by dropping coins in oil containing pot (placed on roads in most Indian towns on Saturdays) bearing statue of Shani Dev as black coloured four-arm figure with a protruding red tongue. Saturn, the planet, is supposed to represent this deity. Worship of Hanuman Ji is understood to offset evil of Shani Dev as Hanuman Ji is known to have defeated Shani on more than one occasion.

Shesh Nag

The serpent god providing itself as the reclining couch with its head as canopy, to Vishnu Ji when he relaxes on ocean surface. Sheshnag, also called Anantnag, does not die when universe is destroyed during pralay and remains Shesh (balance or left over). Shesh Nag is understood to have appeared as brother Balram when Vishnu Ji incarnated himself as Krishn Ji.

Vishwakarma

The celestial architect god and son of Brahma Ji. He is credited with building palaces in heaven, all vehicles of gods and their weaponry. He also built Ravan's golden city of Lanka. Vishwakarma is also known to be the originator of the concept of Vaastu Shastra, taken from Sthapatya Ved, which is relevant to establishing relationship and good order between dweller/dwelling and the cosmos. Knowledge of Vaastu was passed on by Vishwakarma to sages who used it originally in designing of temples.

To his credit also goes the fabrication of Vishnu Ji's Sudershan Chakra and Shiv Ji's Trishul. He was also engaged in building the image of Krishn Ji as Jagannath.

He is the god for all craftsmen and shop-floor workmen who worship him especially on Vishwakarma day by placing their tools before his image, after cleaning them.

Varun Dev

The Vedic god of waves and earlier considered as creator & controller of the universe. Much of the rhythm in the cosmos was said to be controlled by him. Gandiv, the divine bow of Arjun (Pandav of Mahabharat) was given to him by Varun Dev.

He is particularly worshipped by fishermen. But he lost prominence because of curse by sage Utathya whose wife was abducted (and later returned) by Varun Dev.

Vayu Dev

The Vedic god of winds, he purifies air. He is said to be the father of Hanuman Ji (of Ramayan) and Bheem (Pandav of Mahabharat).

Yam

The god of death. Depicted as riding a buffalo and holding a noose, he is responsible for taking away the spirit of a person whose time of death has come. Based on the quality of his/her Karm (deeds), decided by the records maintained by Chitragupt Ji, the person is finally sent to heaven or hell.

A legend associated with Yam is about Savitri & Satyawan in Mahabharat, where Savitri offers prayers to Yam and succeeds in preventing her husband Satyawan from being taken away by Yam, when Satyawan dies. A rare of rarest cases when Yam is shown as being compassionate.

COSMIC CYCLE, AGE OF UNIVERSE AND TIME DIVISION

A. COSMIC CYCLE & AGE OF UNIVERSE A MACRO VIEW·

According to Hindu mythology, universe exists under a certain rhythm and is created, destroyed and recreated in a perpetual cyclic process.

TIME CYCLE TERMED KALP

A time cycle of 4320,000,000 man - years is one day in Brahma Ji's cyclic life and is called Kalp. At the end of this period, the universe is destroyed in a process called Pralay, by way of Brahma Ji absorbing all the worlds into himself before recreation of the universe (his) next day. Different periods within this time cycle, are described in some detail in the following section.

LARGER TIME CYCLE TERMED PARA

A bigger time cycle called Para is 100 years of Brahma Ji's life. This time round, Brahma Ji, alongwith the entire universe gets absorbed into the supreme energy Vishnu Ji. This annihilation is called Mahapralay after which Brahma Ji appears once again on the lotus from the navel of

Vishnu Ji in this cyclic cosmic process.

It may be relevant to reiterate that this time cycle is preceded by as well as followed to, infinity i.e. the absolute beginning and the terminal end are beyond human comprehension.

Present position of existence of the Universe

At macro level, we are presently at a point in time when half the time period of Brahma Ji's one day is over and

at the mircro level, we are in the Kalyug which began about 5000 man-years ago.

Micro level details are given in the following passages.

B. TIME DIVISIONS - A MICRO VIEW

There are different divisions or units of time for men and gods as follows.

Divine-day-equal to one man -year of 360 days based on the fact that there are 360 degrees is one circle. One degree is taken as equal to one day and the complete cycle of earth round sun in 360 days and is related to divine day.

Divine-Year-equals 360 man-years

Yug/Mahayug/Manvantar - During Brahma Ji's one day, one particular universe exits, before it is annihilated through Pralay, followed by recreation of the Universe by him in this cyclic processes mentioned earlier. This passage of time between consecutive Pralays i.e existence of one universe and called Kalp, can be described as consisting of the following.

Manvantar-There are 14 manvantars in one Kalp i.e. Brahma Ji's one day. Each manvantar is reigned by one Manu and is spread over 71 mahayugs, each mahayag consisting of 12000 divine - years or 4320,000 man-years encompassing 4 smaller time spans called yug.

Yug (or Age)-There are 4 different yugs in one mahayug, given sequentially as follows.

Satyug (or Krityug) spanning 4800 divine-years or 1728,000 man-years, a period characterised by all pervading truthfulness & righteousness among humans, a life span of 4000 man-years for humans, a yug where procreation occurs by mere wishing. *Tretayug* spanning 3600 divine-years or 1296,000 man-years when truthfulness which prevailed in the previous Satyug diminishes by 25%, life expectancy down to 3000 years and procreation occurring by a simple touch (let us avoid going into details like who touches whom, when & how etc.)

Duaparyug spanning 2400 divine -years or 864,000 man-years, truthfulness & righteousness diminishing further to 50% of the previous Tretayug

level and procreation achieved through properly organized marriages.

Kalyug spanning 1200 divine-years or 432,000 man-years, truthfulness & righteousness going down to a very low level of 25% of the level prevailing during the previous Duaparyug, charactrized by low character all round, including extra-marital relationships and poor respect for elders and teachers and to rules of society etc.

HINDU CONCEPTS, BELIEFS AND RITUALS

ASHRAMS

meaning stages of life, is a significant concept in Hinduism. According to this concept, a man undergoes four stages in life, namely:
- *Brahmcharya* (bachelorhood)
- *Grahst* (as a married householder)
- *Vanprasth* (leading semi-retired life, studying religious scriptures) and finally.
- *Sanyas* (a life of total renunciation)

AYURVED

a study of human body to remove imbalances between body's three basic forces know as Vat (which controls body's physical and psychological rhythms), Pitt (which controls heat and metabolism) and Kaph (which controls overall structure and stability of the body). Ayurved is based on vedic scriptures & Upvedas (read under chapter on religious literature). According to this science of medicine, optimization of these three forces namely Vat, Pitt & Kaph, through intake of herbs, controlled diet and exercise can lead to good health. Ayurved is the only medical science, which emphasises not only on keeping healthy but also on enhancing life as well. This science was originated by Dhanvantri, the physician god.

BRAHM MAHURT

A point of time just before dawn, considered as best time to wake up. Logically, it is a form of daylight time saving mechanism, facilitating a person to complete his/her ablution and self-cleaning activities, to be ready for worldly activities at dawn when light breaks, ensuring maximum utilisation of daytime sunlight.

DHOTI

white long cloth, usually worn by a person over the body, as a single piece of clothing at the time of performing rituals. It is perhaps to ensure hygiene, as one single piece of cloth, properly washed, can achieve

this more easily, than several pieces of attire, where one or the other piece may not be clean.

CHOTI

small tail of hair at the crown of the head of a person and maintained by devout Hindu males. It provides a cushion to the delicate part of the head, protecting it from any accidental blow.

COW

is accorded a very high status by Hindus. Its milk is highly nutritious and helps to dispel many diseases. Its dung is used for scrubbing floors in households for hygiene and its urine for cure against diseases associated with lever, spleen etc. as it contains mercury and sulphur. It is also believed that all the 330 million gods & goddesses in Hindu mythology, reside in cow. Cow slaughter is therefore against Hindu belief. Cow is a highly protected animal, always addressed by Hindus, as Gau Mata, the mother cow.

DANCES (HINDU)

are a creation attributed to Shiv Ji's Tandav & Lasya dances. This art was later codified in Natya Shastra, by sages. It is all about expression of

emotions by way of body movements, usually accompanied by music. It may be interesting to mention here that dances were initially performed by Dev Dasies (bonded prostitutes in temples).Some of the prominent classical Hindu dance styles are:-
- *Manipuri (Assam)*
- *Bharat Natyam (Tamil Nadu)*
- *Kathakali & Mohiniattam (Kerala)*
- *Kathak (Uttar Pradesh) &*
- *Kuchipudi (Andhra pradesh)*

FASTING

called Vrat or Upvaas, is a matter of imposing certain discipline on eating pattern. It is observed on a number of festivals as also a matter of routine like on certain weekdays. This practice was incorporated alongwtih rituals, with the basic idea of keeping one's physical system healthy. It is interesting to note how selectively some fasts are observed with prohibition on eating rice (to reduce sugar loading in the body) while in some fasts, increased intake of fruits is emphasised (to enhance intake of minerals & vitamins).

GAYATRI MANTRA

the sacred Vedic hymn in praise of Lord Surya as the supreme force, and is known as the mother of all the

vedas. The Gayatri Mantra is :

Om Bhoor bhuvah swah
tat savitur varenyam
bhargo devasya dhimahi
dhiyo yo nah prachodyat

meaning "We meditate on the excellent light of the divine sun. May he enlighten our minds". Later, Gayatri got personified as wife of Brahma Ji.

HAVAN

is a ritual performed by offering some sacred items like ghee (clarified butter), grains etc. to fire, as a matter of propitiating gods for achievement of certain good in the larger interest of family or community.

HOROSCOPE

is a guiding document about the influence of planets and stars on a person and his activities. Most Hindus have faith in this science of astrology and give great importance to horoscopes, which are invariably prepared at the time of birth and consulted by priests for deciding on marriage partners, dates/timing (mahurt- auspicious time) for performing acts like start of a journey, building a house etc.

JANEU

is a sacred thread worn by Hindu males on their body, from the time they reach adolescence. Related ritual is part of the Upnayan Sanskar. This thread is put on the body of the wearer, by the teacher who makes him take certain vows, directed towards concentrating on education & keeping sexual desires suppressed. The sacred thread on the person's body serves as a reminder of those vows. From medical point of view, it also helps in bowel movements, when as per practice, the janeu is put on the right ear so as to facilitate easy release of wastes from the body through pressure on a particular nerve near the ear.

KUMBH

is about large congregation (in millions) of Hindu priests and others taking ritual both together at a pre-determined time of planetary alignment. It is a celebration made four times every twelve years - once, every three years, at each of the following locations.
- *Prayag in Uttar Pradesh (Allahabad)at the confluence of rivers Ganga, Yamuna & the mythical Saraswati*
- *Haridwar in Uttaranchal where river Ganga enters plain*
- *Ujjain in Madhya Pradesh on the banks of river Shipra and*
- *Nasik in Maharashtra, on the banks of river Godavari.*

The one at Prayag, once every twelve years is called Maha Kumbh. When Samudra Manthan was over and the Kumbh containing amrit (nectar) appeared, demons took it away, with the gods chasing them. For twelve divine days, there was a chase and fighting between demons and gods. During this process, drops of amrit fell at four places mentioned above and hence these places and waters therein achieved sanctity.

MALA (ROSARY)

is a set of beads made of wood, cotton, pearls or rudraksh, adequately bound with thread and used as necklace, band on wrist or ankles and more often for facilitating worship or meditation. Rudraksh beads touching the body are claimed to impart physical, intellectual and emotional advantages. Number of beads in a rosary is typically 108, considered an auspicious number by Hindus as it relates to 27 constellations in the entire Zodiac, each constellation being made up of 4 phases. This number i.e 27 x 4 = 108 thus signifies coverage of the entire space, meaning greatness.

MARRIAGE CEREMONY & RELATED RITUALS OF SEVEN PHERE & SAPTAPDI

have two very interesting and significant elements in the entire marriage ceremony, one of the sixteen Hindu *Sanskars*.

a) Seven Phere (perambulations round

sacred fire) at the time of marriage done by the bride & the groom while taking seven vows (like being honest to each other, not hiding anything from each other etc.), one vow for each day, covering seven days of the week and, by extrapolation, covering the entire life. Seven is a sacred number not only for Hindus but in many other religions also. For Christians, the world was created in seven days. For Muslims, they must take seven rounds of Meccas' holy stone.

b) Saptpadi or seven steps ceremony to seek blessings for a prosperous life. Here, the groom makes the bride take seven steps in the north direction, one step each being with a promise from the groom about providing her with wealth, comforts etc.

MEDITATION

is an art of imparting composure and

stability to mind - leading to a subdued state of the mind. There are several methods of doing meditation, such as rhythmic breathing etc.

MOKSH

salvation or liberation for the ultimate union with the Supreme, thereby terminating the cycle of birth-death-rebirth, which is the goal of every Hindu. The belief is about rebirth into lower or higher echelons of the living world, depending upon the quality of karm (deeds) during his/her lifetime. The concept of moksh appeared prominently on the horizon of Hindu philosophy through the influence of Upnishads.According to Hindu scriptures, in this living world, life manifests itself in 8.4 million species in the following classification, in order of increasing levels of consciousness: -

● *Udbhij* (plants growing from soil)
● *Swede Ja* (micro-organisms like bacteria, fungus etc)
● *Anda Ja* (coming to life through egg)

●*Jarayu Ja* (coming to life from womb, such as in case of humans)

MUSIC (HINDU)

employed in bhajans (devotional songs) and other religious activities, it is divided into two categories, namely Hindustani music and Carnatic music. While Hindustani music has its origins in the north and influence of Persian music, Carnatic music has its origins in the south and having its roots in the Vedas (*Gandharv Ved & Upved*) and originally composed by the Gandharvas (celestial musicians). They were influenced by the rhythmic sounds emanating from Shiv Ji's damru (small drum) and Saraswati Ji's lute.

PRALAY

the great deluge and annihilation of the universe occurs at the end of each cosmic cycle. It is heralded by the tandav dance of Shiv Ji. Different types of Pralay are there according to Hindu mythology. These can be discribed briefly as: Pralay - comes at the end of Brahma Ji's each day (about 4300 million man-years) when heaven, earth and the nether world are destroyed. Brahma Ji consumes these worlds into himself, rests during the intervening night and then works again on recreation of the universe next morning (his next morning). This cycle goes on for Brahma Ji's 100 years. Maha Pralay - comes once every 100 years of Brahma Ji. This

time, Brahma Ji, alongwith the three worlds, gets absorbed into Vishnu Ji. Now what remains is only the supreme energy, Vishnu Ji himslef.

RUDRAKSH

is a powerful and sacred bead from tree of a certain species, which grow in Asia. It is claimed to help one achieve physical, intellectual and emotional advantages as well as prosperity. These beads are plucked from the tree, sanctified and energised through certain rituals. Potency of a bead is maintained through regular prayers/rituals. Rudraksh literally means Shiv Ji's tears. According to Hindu mythology, when Shiv Ji was to kill a powerful demon Triparasur, on the request of gods, he knew he will have to use his most powerful weapon Aghor. The very thought of the devastating after-effects of this weapon brought

tears in his eyes. Wherever his tears fell on earth, rudraksh trees grew up at those spots, signifying his eyes.

SANATAN DHARM

is the real term for Hindu faith. It literally means an ever-lasting faith. It is said so because ingrained in this belief are those guidelines, which provide life, conditions of maximum possible existence. This is the Dharm not only for the believers but valid for all human beings, hence its fundamental belief Vasudhaiva Kutumbakam (the whole world is a family).Basic features of this faith are:-

A. Concept of Karm: As you sow, so shall you reap (which incidentally, also gives rise to the belief in the cycle of rebirth by which way, one is accountable to one's acts in previous birth and is rewarded or punished in the next birth)

B. Joint family system: Seniority (by age/relationship) is given more importance and respect and

C. Caste System: Where Brahmans, Kshatriyas, Vaishyas and Shudras are expected to be engaged in specific areas of religion, protecting society, financial and services, respectively.

SELF-CLEANING

an important early morning ablution quite ritually observed by Hindus. This is logically important because of the tropical conditions where lots of sweat and dust can

SINDOOR

is a red coloured powder , applied at the hair parting on the head by Hindu women, as a symbol of fertility. Its red colour is derived from the colour of blood which is an important element of procreation.

SOOTAK

is a time period of a sort of untouchability, akin to quarantine , observed seriously among Hindus at times of birth and death in the family. It is at both such times that emotional disturbances take place and family members must be given time to readjust themselves.

cause diseases. This frequent cleaning of self also includes, washing of hands and feet, with water. Feet of guests are often ceremonially washed when they arrive after traveling distances. Religious bathing ceremonies like Ganga Snan, Kumbh etc. have specifically been positioned in the winter months when natives may otherwise skip baths and deprive themselves of the much needed hygiene.

SHANKH (CONCH SHELL)

is blown by Hindus at prayer and other auspicious times. It has several advantages including good exercise for lungs and the germicidal effect of its sound waves, resulting in repelling of mosquitoes etc.

SHRAADH

a ritual observed by relatives after death of a person, is a show of gratitude towards the dead by offering special food preparations to priests, assuming it will satisfy the dead. Such activities bring to focus the basics of Hindu philosophy where emphasis is more on doing things without hope of a reward - nishkam bhav. For this reason, a Hindu would observe shraadh of the departed one, more seriously, from whom nothing can be expected now, in return, than celebrating the birthday of a young one, from whom material gains are possible in the future. Shraadh is therefore a matter of showing gratitude to the departed, a term dervied from the word shraddha, meaning expression of gratitude.

SWASTIK

called Satiya in Hindi, it is an auspicious sign signifying well being and harbinger of luck because it is understood to be a graphic symbolisation of Ganesh Ji. It is drawn on occasions/places to ensure auspicious beginnings and particularly for ritual ceremonies.

TEERTH YATRA (PILGRIMAGE)

is a journey to places of worship, religious centres and sacred river baths etc, periodically undertaken by Hindus. The basic idea behind this is to traverse the country, know it and ensure solidarity among people of different regions. Teerth literally means a place at the riverside, where most of the pilgrimage centres are located. Kumbh Mela, described in the earlier pages, is one such pilgrimage, which is very popular, attracting millions of Hindus.

TILAK

a mark on the forehead, applied as an auspicious mark which consists of applying roli (red powder) on the forehead and putting some rice grains on it. It is symbolic of regeneration, where roli represents blood and rice grains represent sperms. Regeneration process was treated with great honour in the olden times when infant mortality rate used to be very high.

TULSI

also called Vrinda or Brinda. Legend has it that Tulsi, a woman, prayed intensely for marrying Vishnu Ji, but Lakshmi Ji, fearing rivalry, turned her into a plant. Vishnu Ji, who was deeply impressed with Tulsi's devotion, manifested himself as Shaligram in the form of ammonite (an extinct cuttle-fish like creature having hard shell characterised by a head with arms), now symbolised simply by a black stone.

This manifestation of Vishnu Ji as Shaligram was with the idea of remaining close to Tulsi for all times to come.

Another legend has it that Tulsi plant, symbolises Radha Ji who was married to Krishn Ji. Since the marriage was not legitimate (Krishn Ji being already married to Rukmini Ji) symbolically, Tulsi plant can not enter any home and is kept outside

the threshold. Personifying devotion, Tulsi leaf is an integral part of offerings to gods.

Tulsi (basil) also has several medicinal qualities as established scientifically. It is interesting to note that chewing Tulsi is prohibited, in Hindu scriptures. Logic is that it contains mercury which can cause damage to teeth but when swallowed, the same mercury imparts benefits to the body.

VAASTU SHASTR

is about optimisation and balance between the five elements air, water, fire, earth and space which determine bio-electric magnetism and help ensure wealth, peace and prosperity in a household and other places.

Scientific importance of the balance between the five elements, was realised by sages in the vedic era itself. Based on this understanding, Vaastu Shastr was developed which provided a guide to designing buildings and positioning of its different components such as windows, doors etc. which directly influence cross ventilation, incidence of sun rays etc.

VARN SYSTEM(CASTE)

is a classification among Hindus by caste and a significant feature in Hindu philosophy as mentioned under Sanatan Dharm.

Although a sociological phenomenon which did not exist in pre-vedic times, it has roots in later Hindu scriptures.

Varn system was primarily to differentiate between purity levels of breeds/races as well as to provide an indication to the functions/services to be rendered by people, to the society at large. In Hindu scriptures, including Dharm Shastr by Manu, following castes were named/described, in order of their so-called superiority.

● *Brahmans* produced from God's mouth, to get into scholarly and religious activities

● *Kshatriyas*, produced from God's arms, to perform as warriors.

● *Vaishas*, produced from God's thighs, to get into trading activities and

● *Shudras*, produced from God's feet, to get into service oriented activities.

Untouchables was another caste which was later developed within the society, for carrying night soil, skinning of carcasses etc. This categorisation has become meaningless to most unorthodox and educated people and has since been outlawed and its upliftment is being given priority by the Government. According to one school of thought, origin of this caste is based on the system of outcasting people from their caste whenever anyone violated (bhang) set norms of social behaviour and calling them bhangi.

Sub-castes (Gotra) also developed later, depending upon the gurukul a certain group belonged to (and their descendants), such as Kashyap, Bharadwaj etc. Marriages within one such sub-caste are even now prohibited. There are several theories to

this prohibition, as initiated in those olden times, one being that group heads wanted to eliminate competitions within their community, against themselves for women.

It may be noted that inspite of best efforts of some new age reformers, Hindu society continues to remain in the shakles of the caste system.

VEGETARIANISM

is an important element of Hinduism. To impart purity of mind and body, three rules were pronounced as a guide on food, by philosophers in the vedic era. These are :-

● *Hit bhuk* (eating only what is in one's *hit*, meaning benefit, i.e. conducive to good health).

● *Mit bhuk* (eating quantities which are just sufficient to-*mit*- mitigate hunger i.e moderation) and

● *Rit bhuk* (acquiring food with *reet*, meaning propriety i.e. observing certain rules, primary being about not hurting anyone in the process of acquiring food and through honest means)

Based on these guidelines, vegetables/fruits/grains in moderate quantities were best justified. It may be interesting to note here that although vegetables also belong to the living world (read under Moksh in proceding pages), life in vegetables exists at the lowest level of consciousness and therefore, taking life away from it would cause injury of least intensity.

Apart from this, there is another relevant aspects of food. As per Hindu scriptures, food (like thoughts)can be categorised as:-

● *Satvik* (noble foods like vegetables, fruits, flour of water nuts etc. which help in suppression of animal instinct in humans).

● *Rajasik* (spicy food preparations with lots of clarified butter & condiments which enhance relishing of feelings of sensual enjoyment) and

● *Tamasik* (stale vegetarian foods and all non - vegetarian food preparations having pungent odours which arouse wild feelings & emotions).

As can been seen from the foregoing, vegetarian foods, taken in moderation, best satisfy all the pre-conditions for food that is best for humans.

YOG

is literally a matter of synchronisation of two entities. It is usually associated with mind & body to achieve perfect concentration for successful performance in most human endeavours. It is popularly pronounced and spelled as yoga.

POPULARLY REVERED OR IDOLIZED SAINTS, GURUS & HOLY PERSONALITIES

JHULELAL (10th Century)

River deity and popular Saint of Sindhi community. Sometime in the 10th century AD, Hindus in the Sindh region in the north - west (now in Pakistan) turned to the Vedic river god Varun Dev for protection against conversion by Muslim ruler Mirkshah. Varun Dev is said to have incarnated as son of one Udaichand, and was thereafter called Uderolal1. When placed in cradle, the cradle would swing on its own and he was, thereafter, also called Jhulelal2. He saved Hindus from conversion.

KABIR (1440-1519 AD)

He was a poet saint of Kashi (Varanasi, UP) whose poetry is famous even today. He especially preached that there was no difference between a Hindu and a Muslim and fought against hypocrisy permeating the faiths. His parentage is not known as he was discovered by a Muslim weaver couple, floating on a lotus in a lake near Kashi. He was named Kabir. From childhood, Kabir was inclined towards religious things. He became disciple of a

Hindu guru Ramanand and was loved by both, Hindus and Muslims. He started working on the loom and used to sing devotional songs while working. Since he propagated unity of men and gave importance to creed (unity of thought) and not to caste or religion, orthodox Hindu & Muslim sections tried to discredit him. He believed in Nirgun Bhakti and was against formalities in religion and was thus a revolutionary. His poems were highly critical of

both, mullahs (muslim clerics) and pundits (Hindu priests) as can be noted from the following lines of one of his poems

"Kankar pathar jori ke, masjid lio chunae, Ta charhi mulla baang de, bahira hua Khudae" (With brick and mortar, tall Masjid has been constructed. Mulla goes on top of it and shouts in praise of god. Has his god become hard of hearing?).

MAHAVIR (599-467 BC)

The 24th and the last tirthankar (holy teacher) of Jain community, born as Vardhman, son of a prince in Bihar. At age of 30, he denounced everything, even clothes, since he considered nudity as essential to true saintliness, allowing insects to infest his body. Killing was against his belief. Spending all the time in meditation for thirteen years, he achieved mental isolation from worldly things (Nirvan) and was acclaimed as a tirthankar, a great spiritual leader. He became known as Mahavir. As a Jain reformer, he is credited with the concept of non-ownership and of confession, among Jains.

MEERA BAI (1499-1546 AD)

Considered an incarnation of Radha, Saint Tulsidas and singer Tansen, were her contemporaries. In her formative years, once when she was watching a marriage procession, she asked her mother as to who was her husband. The mother jokingly told her that Krishn Ji was her husband. She grew up with this very belief set in her mind. She would worship Krishn Ji's idol for much of the day as well as give the idol a bath and dress it up. When she was married to Rana of Chittor (Rajasthan) who was son of famous Rana Sanga, she continued with her devotional activities towards Krishn Ji's idol, which was not liked much by her husband and in-laws. They spread rumours about her infidelity resulting in her husband making several attempts to get her killed. But Krishn Ji miraculously saved her every time. A snake sent to her turned into a garland and poison turned nectar by God's grace. Her husband Rana died early and, fed up with the behaviour of her in-laws, she migrated to Brindavan (U.P) and continued with her devotional activities there. Later she settled in Mathura (U.P) and finally went to Kathiawar (Gujarat) where she spent her last days. Her devotional songs in praise of Krishn Ji are very popular even today.

NANAK (1469-1539 AD)

Was the first Guru (Prophet)of Sikhs and a poet who spread message of unity and peace during the tyranni-

cal times of Babar. He was founder of Sikh religion. He sang inspirational songs, collection of which are in Adi Granth, a sacred book for Sikhs. He was instrumental in Hindu-Muslim unity and even Babar, ultimately come to respect him. While Nanak wrote the songs, his disciple Mardana set these to music, both doing community singing. Jap Ji (morning prayers) composed by Nanak and sung by every Sikh, describes different stages through which man traverses to reach eternal bliss. Sohila is a collection of evening prayers, also composed by Nanak. He also coined some notable mantras (hymns) including Vahe Guru.

Nanak is also credited with invention of Gurmukhi characters (a simplification of Sanskrit characters). Granth Saheb, a compilation of hymns by different Gurus and Saints in Gurmukhi is today enshrined in every Gurdawara, the holy place for Sikhs. He was succeeded by Guru Angad, followed by other Gurus-Guru Amardas, Guru Ramdas, Guru Arjun Dev, Guru Hargovind, Guru Har Rai, Guru Har Kishan, Guru Teg Bahdur and finally Guru Gobind Singh.

Guru Arjun the 5th Guru has the credit of establishing Sikhisim as a separate religion. He published the Adi Granth, compilation of compositions of several saints (including Hindu and Muslim saints).However his rising popularity was countered by leading Mughals and then the Hindus, by way of torturing him to death. This gave rise to militancy propagated by his son, the next Guru, namely Guru Hargovind. Finally the 10th Guru, Guru Govind Singh transformed Sikhs into a militant community terming themselves Khalsa and started the tradition of Sikhs adhering to wearing kesh (long hair and beards), carrying kanghi (comb), kirpan (knife), wearing kutchcha (solder's breeches) and karha (steel bracelet).To discard caste system completely, men were given surname Singh and women, Kaur.

PARSAVNATH (872-772 BC)
Was the 23rd tirthankar (holy teacher) of Jains. He was from a Royal dynasty. When he was to be married,

he preferred to go in for meditation in absolute nakedness and andabandon the world. He preached against lust, which was the root cause of greed, adultery, crimes and all other vices. Mahavir followed up and modified Parsavnath's teachings.

RAMKRISHNA PARAMHANS
(1836-1886 AD)
Was a scholar saint who worked towards arousing pride in the cultural richness of Hinduism against a pro-western wave growing at a time-when British supremacy was in vogue and religious conversions were rampant. At the same time, he was very broad-minded. To him, caste system was irrelevant and one god was no different than another god. He spent much of his time in West Bengal (Kali Temple at Dakshineshwar) and was married to Sharda Devi, who became holy mother to Ramkrishn's followers.

SAI BABA OF SHIRDI
(1838-1918 AD)
A personification of spiritual perfection and an epitome of compassion. He lived in Shirdi (Maharashtra). He had a great healing touch and even his simple glance could cure people. There is no authentic record of his early life but when he landed in Shirdi, people recognised his powers and addressed him as Sai (Saint). After initially spending time in meditation under a tree, he moved to a neglected mosque which he named Dwarkamai. According to some devotees, he is god-incarnate. He was common man's god. His benevolence, compassion and other virtues evoked great reverence in people who came close to him. He kept a sacred fire perpetually on (dhuni) and gave its ash as holy token to all who came to him for help and blessings.One legend has it that Sai Baba was an incarnation of Shiv Ji and was born to a Brahman couple Ganga Bhavaria and Devgiri Yamma in village Pathri in AP. As a child, once when he opened his mouth, Shiv Ji could be seen inside. Since then, people started worshipping him. As a young preacher, he propagated equality of Hindu and Islamic religions. This infuriated conservatives of both religions. Fearing harm to him, his mother took him to an orphanage, run by a hermit in a nearby village. After studying there for sometime he proceeded to Shirdi where it is said, he performed several miracles, which made him quite famous.

SURDAS (1478 - 1583 AD)

Was a blind but highly accomplished poet who composed immortal devotional songs in praise of Krishn Ji. Born in 1478 near Delhi and like Tulsidas, he became popular during the reign of Mughal King Akbar. He was born blind and was neglected by his own family, to the extent that by the age of 3 years, his real name was forgotten and he was simply called Sur (blind). He spent much of his time sitting outside his home and would listen to troupes of devotional singers passing by. Impressed with these, he followed a troupe one day but because of his handicap of blindness, he was abandoned by the troupe by a lakeside. There, he would listen to conversation of travellers who would stop at the lake for a while and became worldly-wise, to the extent that he developed an extra sense with help of which, he could make some predictions. He migrated to Brindavan (U.P.).Impressed by such a sense and his technique of writing & singing songs in praise of Krishn Ji, a guru named Vallabhacharya appointed him singer at Krishn Ji's Srinath temple. Even the great singer Tansen in the court of king Akbar used to sing Surdas songs which very much impressed the Mughal Emperor, Akbar.

SWAMI DAYANAND
(1824-1883 AD)

The celebrated Hindu reformer of 19th cenrtury and founder of the Arya Samaj movement.An eminent scholar of Sanskrit and Hindi, he wrote a detailed commentary on comparative religions (Satyarth Prakash-meaning exposition of the meaning of truth), vehemently criticised all the Hindu Puraans and worked against untouchability. Born in rich Zamindar Brahman family of Morvi (Gujrat), he was named Mool Shanker. He was later named as Shuddh Chaitanya by a guru whom he met after running away from home because he did not want to get married.Again he met one Swami Poornanad Saraswati who now named him Swami Dayanad Saraswati. He was 24 years of age by this time. Finally in Mathura, he was taken in the fold of Swami Vrijanand as his guru and under whose influence he vowed to revive Vedic religion.Lecturing from place to place, he reached Mumbai where he established the first Arya Samaj. Later he got great success in Punjab and established Arya Samaj in each town. Establishment of D.A.V Schools/Colleges, Kangri Gurukul etc. are to his credit.

TULSIDAS (1532-1623 AD)

Was a saint poet who is credited with writing of Ram Charit Manas, the popular Hindi version of Valmiki's Ramayan. In fact he is considered an incarnation of Valmiki.Tulsidas was married to Ratnavali whom he loved so much that he could not bear even a day's separation. Once when his wife went to her parent's home, Tulsidas followed and stealthily entered her room at night. His wife felt ashamed of this behaviour and told Tulsidas that if he could develop even half of such love and devotion for Lord Ram Chandr Ji, he would get eternal bliss. Tulsidas took her words to heart and became a saint, devoted to Ram Chandr Ji. He wrote several books, the best known being Ram Charit Manas.

Many other

popularly revered or idolized saints/gurus/holy personalities are also there about whom dedicated books are available.

POPULAR HINDU RELIGIOUS LITERATURE

Hindu religious literature like Vedas & Upanishads are believed to be revealed by God. These are the richest religious literature in the whole world in terms of volume, quality, variety and historical value.

Vedas & Upnishads contain hymns and mythological stories in revelation and discussion of universe and its creator, cosmic order and the evolution of Dharm i.e. rules of social conduct, thereby giving direction towards good social behaviour.

It may be interesting to know that one particular piece of Hindu literature i.e. Mahabharat, is the worlds' most voluminous piece of literature.

Hindu religious literature can be classified as follows:-

SHRUTI

that which is revealed by God and includes):
●Vedas (Rig Ved, Sam Ved, Yajur Ved & Atharv Ved)
●Upnishads (over 100 in numbers) and

SMRITI

that which is interpretation and other findings of the previously

mentioned Shruti, by sages & scholars, as per their own comprehensions, and includes Vedangs (Manu Smriti etc), Purans, Uppvedas etc.

We give in this chapter only a brief introduction to some of the more popular pieces of the great Hindu religious literature.

VEDAS (2500 - 600 BC)

Four Vedas, meaning books of knowledge, were written during a period spread over about 2000 years. Identity of the authors of these Vedas is not known. As mentioned earlier, these are believed to have been revealed by God but, it can be assumed that these were written by Aryan seers and sages, over a very long period of time.

RIG VED

meaning praise of wisdom, is the first and the most important of the 4 Vedas. It is a collection of hymns (mantras). Aryans were worshippers of natural elemental phenomenon i.e. earth, fire, sky, air/space, water etc.

They also imbibed the philosophies of aboriginals about importance of animals as well as Dravidian philosophy about gods. Thus natural elements became gods whose praise is written in these hymns. Aryans also started giving thought to the creation of universe and tried to put these thoughts in hymns. There is talk about the rhythm in the cosmos which evolved the concept of Dharm-rules of social conduct. Also discussed in the Rig Ved is the issue of death and rebirth.

Thus Rig Ved is a documentation of the ideas that evolved amongst people about creation, gods and birth and death. Other 3 Vedas namely Yayur Ved, Sam Ved and Atharv Ved are more about ritual details and reveal the gradual development of related arts and sciences.

UPNISHADS (800 BC onwards) also called vedantas, literally meaning religious dialogues between sages and their disciples. There are over 100 Upnishads about philosophical discussions on the Vedas and compilation of mythological tales etc. Identity of the authors of most of the Upnishads, like in case of Vedas, is again not clear. Upanishads are directed at arousing a person's search for truth in his/her own manner, without imposing any doctrine or any myth to be accepted without thought.

PURAAN (600 BC - 200 AD) Believed to be eighteen in number, 6 each addressed to Vishnu Ji, Brahma Ji & Shiv Ji and termed Satvik, Rajasik and Tamasik Puraans respectively, these were written during the Puraanic or the Epic period and are a collection of lots of detailed tales on gods and their incarnations, which constitute much of the Hindu mythology. Visnnu Puraan , Shiv Puraan etc. are examples.

GITA

Better known as Bhagwad Gita, is the most sacred Hindu religious literature as the sermon given to Arjun by Krishn Ji during the war of Mahabharat. It is the gist of the philosophical and ethical issues contained in the Vedas and Upanishads and described in an interesting and simple way so as to be understandable to common people. Primarily, it is about the relevance and importance of selfless action. Gita's authorship is also ascribed to sage Vyas and was written during the period Mahabharat was also being written.

Gist of Gita called 'Gita Saar' is as under

Whatever happened, happened for good.
Whatever is happening, is happening for good.
Whatever will happen, will happen for good.
Why do you worry? Whom are you afraid of?
Who can kill you? Atma is neither born, nor can it die.
What have you lost, for which you weep?
What did you bring with you, which you have lost?
What did you produce, which has perished?
You did not bring anything when you were born.
Whatever you have, you have received from Him.
Whatever you will give, you will give to Him.
You came empty handed, and you will go the same way.
Whatever is your's today, it was somebody else's yesterday
As it will be somebody else's tomorrow.

The great epics of Hindus, the Mahabharat (Gita included) and the Ramayan were also written during this period.

MAHABHARAT

Enacted in Dwaparyug (corresponding to year 3500 BC) and written around 500 BC, is the world's most voluminous religious epic with Gita as an integral part of Mahabharat. Although credit for writing this epic goes to sage Vyas, it seems that there must have been more authors associated with it, since it must have taken a generation to write such a voluminous epic.

Mahabharat contains stories within stories, including Savitri-Satyawan & Nal-Damyanti etc. which are commonly narrated to children.

THE STORY

Mahabharat is about wars fought between Aryan tribes. There was a famous Kuru dynasty of Hastinapur, a place near Delhi, and it had two scions named Dhritrashtra who was blind and younger Pandu. Pandu was made king because of Dhritrashtra's handicap. Pandu had five sons, Yudhishter, Bheem, Arjun, Nakul and Sahdev, from two wives, Kunti and Madri.

All the five brothers were very capable, particularly Yudhishter with religious disposition, Bheem being tough and a glutton and Arjun a great marksman. Dhritrashtra produced 100 sons called Kauravs, eldest being Duroydhan, who was very wicked and his wickedness was supplemented by his maternal uncle Shakuni, who devised plans and thought of regaining power of the kingdom as they strongly belived that Dhritrashtra, being elder brother, should have been the king, in the first place.

On death of Pandu, Duryodhan felt that he deserved to be made the King and played dirty tricks against the five Pandavs. These tricks included burning of their palace, and a game of gamble. A loss for Pandavs in the gamble led to Kauravs insulting Draupadi, the common wife of Pandavs, by trying to disrobe her in the King's court and ultimately to the exile of Pandavs to the wilderness for 13 years.

In the meantime, Dhritrashtra continued to rule, aided by Bhishm Pitamah (uncle of both, Dhritrashtra and Pandu and respected by all) and the Chief Minister Vidur.

It will be in the fitness of things to add here that Draupadi, a princes, was won as wife by Arjun in an archery contest for marriage (Swayamvar). When the five Pandavs returned to their hideout and announced to mother Kunti that they had brought something special, Kunti carelessly told them to share it equally amongst themselves. Mother's advice was taken in all earnest and Draupadi became common wife to all the five Pandavs.

Another important aspect is that during Draupadi's disrobing, Krishn Ji came to her rescue. Inspite of the best efforts of Kaurav's to disrobe her completely, Draupadi's robe (Sari) became infinitely long and she could not be disrobed completely. She was thus saved from absolute humiliation, by the divine intervention.

When the period of exile was over, Pandavs returned and expressed their right to the throne, Duryodhan refused to give away anything.

This led to the war named Mahabharat, between Pandavs and Kauravs. The war was fought in Kurukshetra (Haryana), about 130 km north of Delhi

Krishn Ji, (the 8th incarnation of Vishnu Ji) who was cousin of Pandavs, joined them as Arjun's charioteer, acting as his friend, philosopher and guide. While at war, Arjun got into a dilemma when the thought came to his mind about killing his own cousins for material gain, that is, the kingdom of Hastinapur.

It is at this juncture that Krishn Ji gives the sermon as scripted in Gita, which is about appropriateness of doing assigned duty without thought of the reward involved. This sermon is described in some details in a piece given in the previous page. The War of Mahabharat lasted 18 days, Kauravs were defeated and Pandavs regained the kingdom. Much of the credit for this victory goes to Krishn Ji for his sermons to Arjun and certain other divine interventions.

RAMAYAN

It was written sometime around year 500 BC by sage Valmiki, much after the Mahabharat, again with the objective of making the ethical and philosophical commandments of the Vedas and Upanishads, interesting and understandable to common man.

Ram Chandr Ji, the 7th incarnation of Vishnu Ji, is the hero of this tale which, according to Hindu mythology, took place near the end of Tretayug. Primarily, it gives lessons in righteousness as demonstrated by Ram Chandr Ji.

Ram Chandr Ji was born to King Dashrath and Queen Kaushalya of Ayodhya (UP), about 500 km east of Delhi. He had three brothers namely Bharat (Son of Queen Kekayi) and Lakshman & Shatrughn (sons of Queen Sumitra).

Ram Chandr Ji won Sita Ji as wife in a contest for marriage (swayamvar), Sita Ji being the princess and daughter of King Janak of a neighbouring state Mithila. She was very chaste and beautiful.

Ram Chandr Ji was to become King but Kekayi wanted her son Bharat to be the King, based on the advice of her wicked maid Manthra. Therefore Kekayi asked King Dastrath to send Ram Chandr Ji to 14 years of exile and make Bharat the King. Much against his wishes, Dashrath did so.

Ram Chandr Ji proceeded to wilderness and Sita Ji & Lakshman went along. Ravan, the ten-headed demon King of Lanka kidnapped Sita Ji and took her to his Kingdom. In the meantime, Hanuman Ji, the monkey god became friendly with (rather devotee of) Ram Chandr Ji and helped him in search of Sita Ji. Alongwith Hanuman Ji's monkey army, Sita Ji was finally rescued and the demon king Ravan killed. At the end the exile period they all returned to Ayodhya. Two sons, Luv & Kush were born to Ram Chandr Ji and Sita Ji.

After Ram Chandr Ji was crowned King, gossip about Sita Ji's chastity were made by some. Sita Ji could not tolerate this and requested mother earth to give her shelter. A split in earth occurred and accommodated Sita Ji inside. It was an illusory act, although.

This tale as Ramlila is enacted every year (in episodes, spread over 11 days) in all villages/towns in India, reminding people about the benefits of righteous behaviour and the ethics and philosophy of life as exemplified by Ram Chandr Ji and Sita Ji.

HINDU *SANSKARS*

Hindu Sanskars, that is sacraments, are religious Hindu rituals aimed at imparting benefits to individuals/society/environment and understood to be visible indicators of one's spiritual grace. Sanskars have been described in vedic literature in detail. Main purpose of sanskars is to make a person, who goes through these, a good component of the society by way of:

●Self-purification (physical, mental & spiritual) and

●Respect of the other elements of the universe, including family, society, environment and above all, the gods.

Religious bias was given to the performance of sanskars to ensure that these are always adhered to, generation after generation. Although some of these sanskars originally prescribed have lost relevance, others continue to be observed in all seriousness in these morden times.

Mostly conducted with the help of pundits and accompanied by hymns, there are at least 16 sanskars which are prescribed to be performed from the time of birth to the time of death.

Suitably catagorized for convenience of readers, these are as follows.

A. PRE-NATAL SANSKARS (BEFOR BIRTH)

1.*GARBHADAN*

●Vedas (Rig Ved, Sam Ved, Yajur Ved & Atharv Ved)

●Upnishads (over 100 in numbers) and

to facilitate conception of a good progeny. This is not observed or performed in modern times as people started feeling shy about it. Otherwise, it is to be performed when would-be mother is in good health and between the 4th & the 14th night after her monthly course.

2. *PUMSAVAN*

to sanctify the foetus. Performed during the 3rd month of pregnancy.

3. *SIMANTONNAYAN*

to keep the pregnant woman in good spirits and deter any evil spirits. Performed in the 4th /5th month of pregnancy, it is symbolically done by parting the woman's hair by her husband.

B. CHILDHOOD SANSKARS

4. *JATKARM*

commencing before severing of the navel cord, to take into consideration issues like selection of room for delivery of the child, giving honey to the new-born by the father and praying for child's long-life

5. *NAMKARAN*

to give name to the new-born, generally on 10th or 12th day after birth.

6. *NISHKARMAN*

to mark the first outing for the child from the maternity room, 3-4 months after birth

7. *ANNAPRASAN*

feeding of the child with solid food for the first time, usually in the 6th month after birth.

8. *CHUDAKARAN*

shaving of head, partly or fully, from the point of view of hygiene, done between 3 to 5 years of age.

9. *KARNVEDH*

piercing of ears done before attaining 5 years of age. , to help prevent medical complications later in life, such as hernia, apart from facilitating individual's decoration with ear rings,

C. EDUCATION RELATED SANSKARS

10. *VIDYARAMBHA*

learning of alphabets in the 5th year

11. *UPNAYAN*

initiating the young individual into society by way of imparting skills relevant to the caste to which one belongs, anytime between the age of 5 and 24 years, depending upon the skill to be acquired, but certainly before marriage.

12. *VEDARAMBHA*

commencing study of vedic literature and other related scriptures, generally in the priestly families and at a guru's place. This is performed immediately after the previously performed upnayan sanskar.

13. *KESHANT*

also called godan sanskar, it is about shaving of facial hair of males, followed by gifting of a cow to the guru (teacher) and a one-year period of austere discipline ensuring brahmcharya (keeping away from sexual desires/acts). It is performed around the age of 16 years.

14. *SAMAVARTAN*

to mark the end of studentship and brahmcharya and return to home from guru's place. Performed around age of 24 years, it is a pre-requisite to a married life later. This sanskar is usually performed in conjunction with the previously observed upnayan sanskar or with the marriage sanskar which follows.

D. HOUSEHOLD LIFE
15. *VIVAH*

the marriage ritual, following which a person leads a family life (grahstashram), performed when a person is grown up to maturity. In case of males, it is done when he achieves economic independence.

E. AFTER DEATH
16. *ANTYESHTI*

funeral ceremony ritually performed by close ones, to ensure easy passage of the dead to the next and supposedly higher world.

OTHER SANSKARS

After the Vivah Sanskar (No. 15 above) and after completion of the active householder life, there are two more sanskars which are not quite popular these days and hence excluded from the preceding passages. These can be enumerated as follows:-

15. A) *VANPRASTH*

commencing sometime after the age of 50 years and when one's worldly responsibilities are over, leading a semi-retired and a simpler life in the study of religious scriptures and

15. B) *SANYAS*

a life of total renunciations, awaiting death. This can commence after 12 to 25 years of commencing the previous vanprasth stage. At this stage, the sacred thread Janeu (worn during the upnayan sanskar) and the tuft of hair on the head (if there) are discarded and saffron clothes put on.

POPULAR HINDU FESTIVALS
(IN CHRONOLOGICAL ORDER OF HINDU/ENGLISH CALENDAR)

Hindu society has many festivals, ceremonies and customs spread all over the year, celebrating change of season, demonstration of respect/love for the spouse/children/parents, welcoming new bride into the household etc, all executed in a rather fancy style. Several objectives were clearly in the minds of our ancestors while designing these. Religious colours were given to these, to ensure that such celebration were adhered to. Providing opportunity for family togetherness and excitement, most of these Hindu festivals are directed towards spiritual purification and characterised by fasting and worship of gods & goddesses and are observed together with family and friends.

Given here are some of the popular Hindu festivals, alongwith dates on which these are observed, as well as the rationale behind the same.

Note : Wherever exact dates are not given, these are decided in accordance with the Hindu Panchang, a system based on lunar cycle and therefore, determined on year to year basis.

LOHRI : JAN. 13
A festival for farmers of north India, particularly Punjab/ Haryana, in celebration of a promising crop, sown earlier in Sept/Oct, that would be completely mature around end March. Celebrations are around bonfire.

PONGAL : JAN. 14
The most important harvest festival for Tamils, in honour of sun & rain gods, celebrated over 3-4 days.

MAKAR SANKRANTI : JAN. 14
To earn a place in heaven after death, by bathing in a river and praying the sun god, the day being considered auspicious according to overall planetary position.

BASANT PANCHMI : JAN/FEB
Prayer & pooja devoted to Saraswati Ji, the goddess of knowledge, coinciding with the time when winter is getting over in the north.

MAHA SHIVRATRI : FEB/MAR
A festival celebrating the marriage of Shiv Ji & Parvati Ji. Women pray for prosperity in married life. It is a particularly important festival for Kashmiries.

HOLI : FEB/MAR
There is no religious aspect to Holi. People are cheerful after crops which have been cut & sold, and lots of money available. They play with colours and put these on faces of each other. One mythological story is associated with Holi. When Hiranyakashipu wanted to kill his son Prahlad (also see page 42), he ordered his sister Holika to sit on the fire with Prahlad since Holika was blessed with a boon that she can not get burnt. But surprisingly Holika died while Prahlad came out unscathed. This event is celebrated by burning bonfires, on the day preceding Holi.

SHIVRATRI : JAN/FEB
This is in worship of Shiv Ji

BHAIDOJ : FEB/MAR & OCT/NOV
This Festival occurs twice a year, following Holi & Diwali when married women go to their parental home for sometime and get a chance to get together with the family.

RAM NAVMI : MAR/APR
This is in celebration of the birth of

Ram Chandr Ji, the 7th incarnation of Vishnu Ji.

BAISAKHI : APRIL 14

A festival of north India, it is all about thanking god for the year's first crop i.e Rabi. For Sikhs, it is a special day when their 10th Guru, Guru Gobin Singh initiated 'Panch Pyaras'. On this day, water is brought from various holy rivers and poured into the holy Sarovar at Hari Mandir (Golden Temple, Amritsar).

NIRJALA EKADASHI : JUNE

Ekadashi comes once every 15th day - on the 11th day of waxing moon as well as on the 11th day of waning moon. Observing fast and doing charity on these days is understood to absolve one of any sin committed during the proceding fortnight days.

This exercise twice a month was later changed to a stricter one i.e. fasting without water (nirjal) only once a year. It is also common that while people do not take water themselves, they establish water-dispensing kiosks (Pyao) for the poor, providing them sweetened cold waters. It is said that the custom of observing Nirjala Ekadashi once a year (instead of 24 ordinary Ekadashies) was first introduced by Pandav Bheem (of Mahabharat) who, being a glutton, found it more convenient.

GURU POORNIMA : JULY

This is in worship of sage Vyas who scripted Mahabharat and who was

the original Guru on Vedas. Symbolically, all teachers, parents and elders are extended special respect on this day to seek their blessing, considering them gurus in their own right.

SINDHARA : JULY/AUG

It is a festival for daughters-in-law when sweets/fruits are sent to their parent's home where the daughter-in-law is sent a day earlier. This is more importantly observed in the north, particularly in Delhi,

Gujarat and Rajasthan.

TEEJ : JULY/AUG

Like Sindhara is for daughters-in-law, Teej is for daughters of the household.

RAKSHA BANDAHAN (Saluno) : JULY/AUG

It is a rather sentimental festival where ties between brothers and sisters are restrenthened. Symbolically sisters tie a thread (Rakhi) on the wrist of the brother and the understanding is that he will always strive to protect her.

JANAM ASHTMI : JULY/AUG

To celebrate the birth of Krishn Ji in the Mathura prison one night & in safe custody of Nand & Yashoda in Gokul, next day.

GANESH CHAUTURTHI&
CHOWK CHAKNI : AUG/SEP

It is community pooja of Ganesh Ji where his idol is worshipped and finally immersed in sea or river. It is celebrated more enthusiastically in Maharashtra. In the North, an off-shoot festival Chowk Chakni is celebrated as a festival for boys who receive clothes, small wooden rods (Chatiye), pencils and sweets from maternal grandmother's home.

ONAM : AUG/SEP

In Kerala, it is in celebration of the return of king Bali (of Kerala's golden period) to his land once a year as granted by Vishnu Ji (read details under Vishnu Ji's 5th incarnation page 43)

DURGA POOJA (NAVRATRI / DEVIAN): MAR/APR & SEP/OCT

Durga Ji, a manifestation of Maa Shakti and as wife of Shiv Ji, is worshipped twice a year by way of Durga Puja for nine days each time. According to legend when demon Mahishasur was causing trouble for gods, they prayed Maa Shakti to save them. She appeared as Durga and killed Mahishasur and other demons. It is in honour of this that Durga Pooja is celebrated. Reason for its celebrations twice a year is that Ram Chandr Ji, when going to war against. demon King Ravan, wanted to pray Durga Ji for support and could not wait for Durga Puja time to come. He did so at that very time (March). Thus started the custom of celebrating Durga Puja twice a year. While puja during Mar/Apr. is more of a private affair and done at home, the pooja during Sep/Oct is done more on a community basis with great pomp and show, more particularly in Bengal. Idols of Durga Ji are immersed in water, at the end of the 9-days celebrations.

DUSSEHRA/VIJAY DASHMI : SEP/OCT

It is the last day of the 10- days war, the day on which Ram Chandr Ji killed demon King Ravan. Ramayan is enacted in many places in most cities/towns. On the Dussehra day, effigies of Ravan, Kumbhkaran (brother of Ravan) and Meghnad (son of Ravan) are burnt.

KARVA CHOTH : OCT/NOV

It is the most important festival for Hindu women in the north, when they fast the whole day without food/water, for long life of their husbands. Fasting, which commences before sunrise, is preceded by eating some snacks (sargai). Late in the evening, moon is worshipped, followed by dinner.

DIWALI : OCT/NOV

This is celebrated in honour of Ram Chandr Ji who had earlier returned to Ayodhya after his victory over Ravan, coinciding with the end of the 14 year exile. It is celebrated with fireworks and lighting of homes. This day also marks the worship of goddess Lakshmi Ji.

CHRONOLOGY

OF SOME IMPORTANT MYTHOLOGICAL EVENTS & OTHER SIGNIFICANT HISTORICAL DEVOLOPMENTS IN INDIA DURING THE CURRENTLY EXISTING WORLD
TO GIVE SOME IDEA OF DEVELOLPMENTS AND HOW GODS/MAN HAVE PROGRESSED ON THE TIME SCALE

PERIOD OF COSMIC CYCLE	CORRESPONDING MAN-YEAR (APPROX.)	SOME IMPORTANT EVENTS
BEGINNING	4000 mn. years BC	PRALAY - the great deluge, marking end of the previously existing universe.
SATYUG	4000mn. BC-20000 BC (STONE AGE)	1st INCARANATION OF VISHNU JI- as fish Matsya to restore Vedas. UNIVERSE CREATED -by Brahma Ji and its evolution takes place including development of gods, man, demons, animals etc. SAMUDRA MANTHAN- by gods & demons and discovery of several celestial and other things 2nd INCARNATION OF VISHNU JI -as tortoise Kurma to hold earth on his back during Samudra Manthan. 3rd INCARNATION OF VISHNU JI -as Varaha the boar, to rescue earth on his tusks during a deluge caused by demon king Hiranykash. 4th INCARNATION OF VISHNU JI - as Narasimha to save devotee Prahlad from atrocities of his father, demon king Hiranyakashipu. 5th INCARNATION OF VISHNU JI - as Vaman, the dwarf to restore heaven to gods, from demon king Bali. 6th INCARNATION OF VISHNU JI - as Parshuram to counter oppression caused by Kshatriya kings.
TRETAYUG	(20000 BC- 10000 BC) (STONE AGE)	7TH INCARNATION OF VISHNU JI - as Ram Chandr Ji, born to king Dashrath of Ayodhya (U.P.) ENACTMENT OF RAMAYAN
DUAPARYUG	(10000 BC - 3102 BC) (STONE AGE)	8TH INCARNATION OF VISHNU JI -as Krishn Ji in Mathura (U.P.)

KALYUG	(3101 BC - to date)	ENACTMENT OF MAHABHARAT
VEDIC PERIOD (2500 -600 BC)	(BRONZE AGE- 2500-1200 BC) (Iron Age - 1200BC-1740AD)	COMPOSITION OF VEDAS BIRTH OF LORD PARSAVANTH COMPOSITION OF UPNISHADS
EPIC PERIOD (600 BC - 200 AD)	600 BC-TO-200 AD	9th Incarnation of Vishnu Ji - as Buddh· GITA COMPOSED by sage Vyas and others MAHABHARAT COMPOSED by sageVyas and others. RAMAYAN COMPOSED by sage Valmiki
ANCIENT PERIOD	950 AD 1440 AD 1469 AD 1478 AD 1499 AD 1532 AD (Industrial Revolution 1740AD-1900AD)	JHULELAL born KABIR - spreads message against religious orthodoxy in different religions NANAK - the first Sikh Guru and the founder of Sikh religion is born SURDAS - composes songs in praise of Krishn Ji. MEERA - composes devotional songs in praise of Krishn Ji. TULSIDAS -writes Ram Charit Manas
MODERN TIMES	1836 AD 1838 AD	RAMAKRISHN PARAMHANS - arouses pride in Hindu culture against growing influence of West SAI BABA OF SHIRDI - performs several miracles and blesses many people

Note :-

1. It is believed that Vedas existed earlier and were rescued by Vishnu Ji in his 1st incarnation. These were recited by gods to sages. Later, these are believed to have been written/documented by Aryan scholars during the Vedic period.

2. Most of the Upnishads were written/documented during 800-600 BC. However, some Upnishads have been written later also.

AN IDEA OF THE
HINDU CALENDAR

VIKRAM SAMVAT

Hindus generally follow the Vikram Samvat. Named after King Vikramaditya, it came into being, 57 years ahead of the Christian Era. The Hindu year begins in Chaitr, and counted from the Samvatsara Parv, the first day of the waxing moon in the month of Chaitr. Twelve months of the Hindu Calendar and their equivalent in the Gregorian Calendar are as under :-

MONTHS

1 CHAITR----------------------------Mar-Apr
2 BAISAKH-------------------------Apr-May
3 JYESHTH-------------------------May-Jun
4 ASHADH---------------------------Jun-Jul
5 SHRAVAN (SAWAN)--------------Jul-Aug
6 BHADRAPAD(BHADON)-------Aug-Sep
7 ASHVIN----------------------------Sept-Oct
8 KARTIK---------------------------- Oct-Nov
9 MARG SHEERSH ----------------Nov-Dec
10 PAUSH----------------------------Dec-Jan
11 MAGH-----------------------------Jan-Feb
12 PHALGUN (PHAGUN)---------Feb-Mar

DAYS

1 PRATIPADA--1st day of lunar fortnight
2 DWITEEYA---------------------Second day
3 TRITEEYA-----------------------Third day
4 CHATURATHI-----------------Fourth day
5 PANCHAMI----------------------Fifth day
6 SHASHTHI----------------------Sixth day
7 SAPTAMI----------------------Seventh day
8 ASHTAMI---------------------Eighth day
9 NAVAMI------------------------Ninth day
10 DASHAMI---------------------Tenth day
11 EKADASHI-----------------Eleventh day
12 DWADASHI------------------Twelfth day
13 TRIYODASHI-----------Thirteenth day
14 CHATURDASHI -------Fourteenth day
15th day of bright fortnight is called Poornima while the fifteenth day of dark fortnight is called Amaavasya.

Each fortnight is called paksh
Normally each day has its significance but Ekadashi and Poornima are generally held very auspicious.
The days called tith, are based on relative motion of earth with respect to Sun & the Moon. This means that each tith does not comprise exactly of 24 hours but can vary by some hours. As such, a particular tith can fall on two consecutive days and sometimes, a tith can even miss a Calander date of the Gregorian Calander . In simple words, say, an Ashtmi can be shown on two consecutive dates and, say, a Panchmi, may find omission with Chaturthi followed by Shashthi

WEEKDAYS
1.SOMVAAR
(Devoted to Shiv Ji) Monday
2.MANGALVAAR (Devoted to Hanuman Ji) Tuesday
3.BUDHVAAR
(Devoted to Vishnu Ji) Wednesday
4.BRAHSPATIVAAR
(Devoted to Ganesh Ji/Sai Baba) Thursday
5.SHUKRAVAAR
 (Devoted to Shiv Ji/ Devi Ji) Friday
6.SHANIVAAR
(Devoted to Hanuman Ji/ Shani Dev) Saturday
7.RAVIVAAR
 (Devoted to Surya Dev) Sunday
Note : However, it may be noted that week is not an original Hindu concept where sub-unit of month is a fortnight (Paksh) as described earlier.

SEASONS

According to the ancient Hindu Calendar, there are six seasons, each comprising of two months.

1.VASANT ---------------------------- Spring
Comprising Chaitr - Baisakh
2. GREESHM------------------------Summer
Comprising Jyeshth - Ashadh
3. PAAVAS-- --------------------Rainy Season
Comprising Shravan - Bhadrapad
4.SHARAD----------------------------Autumn
Comprising Ashvin - Kartik
5.HEMANT----------------------Mild Winter
Comprising Marg Sheersh-Paush
6. SHISHIR----------------------------Winter
Comprising Magh - Phalgun

Inconsistency between solar and lunar calendar due to the fact that there are only 354 days in the 12 months lunar cycle, is taken care of in the Indian Calendar by way of an Adhik Mas (additional month) after every thirty lunar months. This adhik mas (leap month) generally falls after Ashadh or Shravan and is termed second Ashadh or second Shravan.Another notable difference between Gregorian and Vikram Calendar is that while in Vikram Calendar, transition of the sun always takes place around 14th or 15th of a month (month of Gregorian Calendar), in the Gregorian Calendar it is on 20th or 21st of the month.
Equivalent Zodiac signs are given below, as a piece of relevant information:-

1. Aries------------------------------------Mesh
2. Taurus----------------------------------Vrish
3. Gemini--------------------------------Mithun
4. Cancer----------------------------------Kark
5. Leo--------------------------------------Sinh
6. Virgo----------------------------------Kanya
7. Libra------------------------------------Tula
8. Scorpio----------------------------Vrishchik
9. Sagittarius--------------------------Dhanu
10.Capricorn---------------------------Makar
11. Aquarius-------------------------Kumbh
12. Pisces--------------------------------Meen

DICTIONARY OF IMPORTANT/RECURRING WORDS IN THE TEXT

Absolute	-complete, perfect & pure
Atma	-soul, the spiritual or material part of living beings
Avataars	-incarnation, an embodiment of eternal gods in mortal form
Brahmand	-cosmos or universe, the whole and infinite creation consisting of galaxies, living beings and all material things.
Cosmic	-pertaining to the universe
Devnagri	-the script for writing some Indian languages
Divine	-pertaing to God
Dharm	- faith, belief in religious doctrines which provide a guide to character and conduct of humans.
God	-supreme energy as creator & ruler of the universe whose several manifestations/images have appeared over time (imagined or otherwise) for worship by humans.
Guru	-teacher, particularly a spiritual teacher
Hermit	-religious person living in solitary retirement
Hindu	-people living beyond (east & south) Sindhu (Indus) river in the north of the Indo-Gangetic plain, the word distorted by Persians, from Sindhu to Hindu.
Hindusim	-the religion followed by Hindus, a religion guided by religious scriptures like Vedas, reflecting on their social, cultural and philosophical activities.
Legend	-traditionally popular mythical stories
Monotheism	-doctrine that there is only one God, the supreme power
Myth	-fictitious and usually primitive tales involving supernatural characters, embodying popular ideas pertaining to historical or natural phenomenon.
Mythology	-collection of myths prevailing in a geographical region
Nether world	-lower world, usually associated with demons
Puraan	-religious literature giving tales pertaining to Hindu mythology
Sage	-profoundly wise person
Saint	-holy person, highly revered in human society.
Sanskar	-sacrament, religious Hindu rituals aimed at imparting benefit to individuals/ society /environment and understood to be visible indicators of one's spiritual grace.
Sanskrit	-the ancient language of Hindus in India in which much of the Vedic literature was written, also the oldest member of the Indo-European family of languages.
Seer	-a visionary, typically from the holy fraternity .
Scripture	-a sacred original writing .
Trimurti	-trinity, literally a group of three but in reference to Hinduism, it is an immense energy comprising three eternal gods, namely Vishnu Ji, Brahma Ji and ShivJi.
Vedas	-the oldest and sacred Hindu literature written in Sanskrit language.
Upnishads	- philosophical discourses documented in scriptures, based on Vedas.
Yug	-specific and long time period or age